W9-AQX-501
OHIO DOMINICAN
COLLEGE LIBRARY
COLUMBUS, OHIO
43219

TWAYNE'S WORLD AUTHORS SERIES

A Survey of the World's Literature

Sylvia E. Bowman, Indiana University

GENERAL EDITOR

RUSSIA

Nikolai Nekrasov

(*TWAS 19*)

TWAYNE'S WORLD AUTHORS SERIES (TWAS)

The purpose of TWAS is to survey the major writers —novelists, dramatists, historians, poets, philosophers, and critics—of the nations of the world. Among the national literatures covered are those of Australia, Canada, China, Eastern Europe, France, Germany, Greece, India, Italy, Japan, Latin America, New Zealand, Poland, Russia, Scandinavia, Spain, and the African nations, as well as Hebrew, Yiddish, and Latin Classical literatures. This survey is complemented by Twayne's United States Authors Series and English Authors Series

The intent of each volume in these series is to present a critical-analytical study of the works of the writer; to include biographical and historical material that may be necessary for understanding, appreciation, and critical appraisal of the writer; and to present all material in clear, concise English—but not to vitiate the scholarly content of the work by doing so.

Nikolai Nekrasov

By M. B. PEPPARD

Amherst College

Twayne Publishers, Inc. :: New York

Copyright © 1967, by Twayne Publishers, Inc.
All Rights Reserved

Library of Congress Catalog Card Number: 67-12266

891.7
N418P

MANUFACTURED IN THE UNITED STATES OF AMERICA

Preface

THE works of the great Russian prose writers have long been part of our own intellectual heritage. Dostoevsky and Tolstoy, Turgenev and Chekhov have taken their place in our reading lists and are known to a wide audience. The Russian poets have fared less well, and in spite of translators' efforts Pushkin and Lermontov are poets whose names are widely known but whose works are little read. Yet their fame, if not their poetry, has reached us, whereas the name Nekrasov suggests little to anyone but a few émigrés and graduate students.

This neglect is all the more regrettable in view of the great importance of Nekrasov in Russian literary history. Nikolai A. Nekrasov was not only a great and popular poet whose place in Russian literature is next to that of the famous classic poets mentioned above, but also a famous and important publisher. He was the first publisher of both Dostoevsky and Tolstoy, and was for many years both the publisher and close friend of Turgenev. For nearly thirty years, from 1847 to 1877, he was editor of the leading literary periodical of the day. He was the first to provide the great critic Belinsky with his own and proper forum in *The Contemporary*. In the 1850's and 1860's he performed the same important service for the critics Chernyshevsky and Dobroliubov, the great satirist Saltykov-Shchedrin, as well as for many less well-known authors. It was in the pages of *The Contemporary* that the so-called natural school, the socially critical Realism based on Gogol, found its first support. Since it was first of all as a publisher and propagandist that Nekrasov established his fame, this side of his activities will receive some attention in our book.

While an older school of literary historians saw in Nekrasov's journalism his greatest contribution to Russian letters, it is his

77108

poetry which has endured and which ensures him his prominent position in the history of Russian literature. His poems, well received in the 1840's and 1850's, captured the imagination of the radical youth of the 1860's and 1870's, and from that time on he has held a high place in the hearts of all Russians. Much of his poetry has been learned by heart by generations of school children. Some of his poems have even become "folk poems," recited and passed on by oral tradition. Already in the nineteenth century some of his popularity was due to his themes and subject matter, his sympathy for the suffering serfs and his castigation of the exploiting landowners, rather than to the artistry of his verse. This misunderstanding is persistent and recurrent and has been inherited by the Soviets, who have adopted him as an eloquent precursor of their regime, frequently for the wrong reasons. Nekrasov's position in literary history has often owed as much to an interpretation of his political views as to his literary gifts. But even this misconception is now giving way in the Soviet Union to a growing appreciation of the poet for his artistic achievements.

The growth and development of Nekrasov's mastery of verse is the central theme of this book. We shall consider him both as the heir of a great verse tradition and as innovator and precursor of later developments. Parnassian poets, advocates of "pure poetry," have always recoiled from Nekrasov's didacticism and what was felt to be social or political propaganda. Contemporaries like Turgenev, Tiutchev, and Fet were harshly critical of what they termed the prosiness of his verse. The enthusiastic response of the revolutionary youth to his poems only served to confirm their suspicion that he was primarily a propagandist. Nekrasov's own love of combat and polemics did not help to dispel this view. In his poems he often reproached himself for not being an activist in politics and social reform, a form of self expression which did not endear him to the proponents of detached, "pure" poetry. As he wrote to L. Tolstoy in 1856, the role of the writer is "to be first of all a teacher, and as far as possible, a representative for the humble and voiceless." It was not until the 1920's that the Formalists rediscovered Nekrasov as a *poet*, as a master of form and a consummate artist. Since then the discussion of his relation to Pushkin, with whom he was often put in false opposition, can be carried on reasonably and without tiresome polemics. It is now possible to discuss both his formal achievements and his themes calmly and objectively.

But perhaps it is wrong to speak of his "themes," for Nekrasov may be said to have had one single great theme: Russia—Russia in all its aspects—its strengths and weaknesses, its landscape in all its moods, it people at work and at play, in sorrow and in joy. Nekrasov is, of all Russian writers, the most quintessentially Russian; his themes and subjects are always about Russians and addressed to Russians. For American readers this obviously presents difficulties, yet it is all the more rewarding to study a writer whose nature is so profoundly Russian and whose influence on Russian intellectual life is of such great importance.

Most of the great movements in Russian intellectual and political life during the middle nineteenth century find a direct reflection in the works of Nekrasov. We must therefore be concerned with the history of the period as well as with certain aspects of the poet's career as influential publicist and intellectual. While most of our attention will be focused on those poems which have become the foundation of his enduring reputation, references to the opinions of other writers, especially such well-known authors as Turgenev and Dostoevsky, have been included where they seemed interesting and pertinent. We hope that this will help the student who has already started in Russian literature to locate Nekrasov more readily. We have concentrated on Nekrasov's public career and have cited his private life only when it bears directly on his work as poet or publicist. This is not, therefore, a biography in the usual sense of the term. The book is organized as follows. Chapter 1 discusses his development as a writer in general terms, combining references to some of the important influences of his early years with a characterization of the main lines of his work and his basic modes of thought. Chapter 2 deals with his beginnings as a critic and publisher, and follows his career in these fields until his death. Chapters 3 through 5 present a discussion of his poems, divided for convenience into three groups: the poems from 1845 to 1856 contained in the first collected poems of *Verses*, 1856; the following ten years until the closing down of *The Contemporary* in 1866; and the works of his final years until his death in 1877. Within these three chapters we have proceeded chronologically within our own grouping of the poems into arbitrary categories. Chapter 6 summarizes his achievement and surveys his position in Russian letters.

M. B. PEPPARD

Amherst College

Acknowledgments

It is a pleasure to acknowledge my indebtedness to Mr. Alfred Kuhn of the Amherst College Russian Department. Without his encouragement this project would never have been undertaken. To Sue K. my thanks are due for coffee, cordiality, and encouragement. Professor Peter Czap of the Amherst College History Department has been most helpful, contributing, correcting, and criticizing.

Contents

Chronology

1821 November 28. Nikolai Alexeyevich Nekrasov born in the village of Nemirov, in the district of Podolia, the son of army lieutenant Alexei Sergeyevich Nekrasov and Elena Andreyevna N., daughter of the landowner Zakrevsky.

1824 Father retired with the rank of major. The family moved to the village of Greshnevo in the district of Iaroslavl.

1824–1832 Grew up on family estate. His father a brutal serf-owner; his mother a delicate and refined lady. Played with serfs a great deal, came to know their life well.

1832 With his older brother Andrei visited the gymnasium in Iaroslavl.

1838 In July death of brother Andrei. July 20 left for St. Petersburg to enter military service. In the city soon began study for the university, which led to break with father. In the fall the publication of two poems in periodicals.

1839 More poems published. Without support from father, forced to live in cellars and flophouses, make his way under great privations; suffered hunger and cold and came to know the lower depths of St. Petersburg.

1840 Early in the year his first collection of poems appeared, *Dreams and Sounds.* In February, became a contributor to a periodical, began to earn a little money. First prose works and vaudevilles appeared.

1841 Contributed poems, reviews, and vaudevilles to periodicals. In July death of his mother. In the fall became contributor to *Notes of the Fatherland,* the periodical in which Belinsky was the leading figure.

1842–1843 Translated comedies and vaudevilles published. In 1843 his first attempt at editing an almanac. Started *Life and Adventures of Tikhon Trostnikov.* Published reviews and bibliographies in periodicals; also some poems.

1844 During summer lived with Belinsky. In the fall edited and published *Physiology of St. Petersburg* containing among other things his story "The Corners of St. Petersburg."

1845 Continued *Physiology of St. Petersburg,* second part containing some of his poems. In the summer persuaded Belinsky to leave *Notes of the Fatherland.*

1846 Published his *Petersburg Collection,* with some of his poems and contributions by Belinsky, Herzen, Turgenev, Grigorovich, Dal, Dostoevsky, Panayev, and others. First censorship difficulties. The secret police add him to their list. Decision to edit and publish his own periodical. Contract with Pletnëv, the owner of *The Contemporary* signed in October. The professor and censor A. V. Nikitenko to be the nominal editor.

1847 In January the first issue of *The Contemporary* under the new editorship. During the year several poems of Nekrasov's published.

1848 Severe repressive measures of the Russian government as a reaction to the revolutions in Europe. Increasing difficulties with censorship. In May Belinsky died. Beginning of the novel *Three Countries of the World.*

1849 Secret police continue observation. In November, he and Panayev summoned by the police.

1851 In January, *The Contemporary* begins to publish the novel *Dead Lake.* Financial difficulties, constant struggle with censorship.

1852 In August, Leo Tolstoy's *Childhood* published in *The Contemporary.*

1853 In the fall first acquaintance with N. G. Chernyshevsky, from now on a contributor to *The Contemporary.*

1855 The "Notes on Periodicals," written together with Botkin, begin to appear. First acquaintance with Dobroliubov. First meeting with Tolstoy.

1856 In the spring a contract with Turgenev, Tolstoy, Ostrovsky, and Grigorovich for the exclusive rights to publish them in *The Contemporary.* In August before leaving for abroad the directorship of the periodical assigned to Chernyshevsky. In October appeared Nekrasov's second collection of poems, *The Poems of N. A. Nekrasov,* very successful in spite of repressive censorship. Travel abroad.

1857 Paris, Rome, Naples. In London to see Herzen, who refused to receive him. In June return to Russia. Dobroliubov full member of the staff of *The Contemporary,* in charge of reviews and bibliography.

1858 Abrogation of the "exclusive contract" with Turgenev and others.

1859 Addition of the satirical section "The Whistle" to *The Contemporary,* edited chiefly by Dobroliubov. In the spring attacks on Nekrasov by Herzen.

1860 Turgenev requested Nekrasov to prevent the publishing of adverse criticism of his novel *On the Eve* by Dobroliubov. After publication of the article beginning of the break with Turgenev. Continued attacks by Herzen.

1861 February 19 the manifesto concerning the emancipation of the serfs. In August the poem "The Pedlars" completed in Greshnevo. In the fall the poem republished in special, cheap popular edition. November 17 death of Dobroliubov.

1862 I. I. Panayev's death February 18. In March Nekrasov confirmed as the sole editor-publisher of *The Contemporary.* June 19 the publishing of the periodical suspended for eight months. July 7 Chernyshevsky arrested. November 30 death of the poet's father.

1863 In February the third edition of *The Poems of N. A. Nekrasov.* In March purchase of a small estate "Karabikha" near Iaroslavl. Final break with A. I. Panayeva, who for years had been his common-law wife.

1864 In January "Red-nosed Frost" published in *The Contemporary.* Fourth edition of the *Poems* published. Continued work on "Who can be Happy in Russia?"

1865 In November preliminary warning of closure from the office of the censor. Publication of the poem "The Railroad."

1866 The prologue to the poem "Who can be Happy in Russia?" published. In April D. Karakozov's assassination attempt on the life of Czar Alexander II. Arrest of the co-editor of *The Contemporary* G. Z. Eliseyev. In June its publication suspended indefinitely.

1867 In the spring spent a few months abroad. In December completion of the contract giving Nekrasov the redactional rights to the periodical *Notes of the Fatherland.*

1868 January the first issue of *Notes of the Fatherland* under Nekrasov's editorship. M. E. Saltykov-Shchedrin became co-editor in June. In November the fifth edition of *Poems* began to appear.

1869 In January the first chapter of "Who can be Happy in Russia?" appeared, second and third chapters follow in February. In April abroad to Paris and German spas. At the end of the year Zinaida Nikolaevna became his common-law wife. (Real name: Fekla Anisimovna Viktorova.)

1870 In February fourth and fifth chapters of "Who can be Happy in Russia?"

1871 During the summer in Karabikha start of the work on "Russian Women."

1872 In April "Princess Trubetskaya" appeared. During the summer continued work on the second part of the poem. In October financed a village school for Greshnevo.

1873 In January "Princess Volkonskaya" appeared. In the summer travel abroad.

1874 The third part of "Who can be Happy in Russia?" appeared in *Notes of the Fatherland.*

1875 Much of the year spent in Karabikha; first signs of his illness.

1876 Travels in search of cure for growing illness. Censorship prevented publication of last part of "Who can be Happy in Russia?" Beginning of composition of "Last Songs."

1877 In January the last will and testament drawn up. Eight poems of the cycle "Last Songs" in *Notes of the Fatherland.* In February the poet received a delegation of students and a testimonial address signed by hundreds of students. In March added a codicil to his will so that Chernyshevsky and family could receive a percentage of the income from the poet's works. In April married Zinaida. In June a visit from Turgenev and a reconciliation. Died December 27; buried December 30. At his grave addresses were given by F. M. Dostoevsky, G. V. Plekhanov, and others.

Note: all dates given in the Old Style. For comparison his birth date in New Style is December 10, 1821, the date of his death January 8, 1878.

CHAPTER 1

The Muse of Vengeance and Grief

> You are destitute,
> You are rich,
> You are weak,
> You are powerful,
> O Mother Russia! (III, 390)[1]

THESE lines from "Who Can Be Happy in Russia?" might be considered as a motto to all the works of Nekrasov, for they express both his sense of Russia's suffering and his high hopes for a better future. For those who suffered, Nekrasov felt pity and grief, and on those who prevented Russia from realizing her greatness and power he demanded vengeance. This lyric cry comes from a poet who was born into the relative comfort and ease of a landowning family. His parents were of the gentry without belonging to the titled nobility. The impressionable years of his youth were spent in play with the children of serfs on the banks of that most Russian of rivers, the Volga. In later years, recalling without sentimentality the period of his youth, the contrast between the privileged brutality of his father and the sordid suffering of the serfs evoked the following lines of characteristic compassion:

> O bitterly, bitterly I wept
> When that morning I stood
> On the bank of my native river
> And first did call it
> The river of slavery and sorrow!

His home lay along the road which the exiles to Siberia traveled, and the tears of the serfs, whom his father used to beat unmercifully, mingled with the doleful chants of the *burlaki,* the Volga "boatmen." His mother, a refined and sensitive woman, suffered under the harsh home life, which was dominated by her ignorant and callous husband. Nekrasov always conceived of his muse in the form of a woman: a composite figure, in part his mother, in part an idealized young peasant woman. His sorrow is for woman's hard lot in life, for the poet knew both the grief of an aristocratic lady like his mother and that of a peasant woman such as Dar'ia of "Red-nosed Frost."

Nekrasov's first awareness of the world was linked with violent contrasts in the social structure of early nineteenth-century Russia. He despised slavery and condemned in bitter and satiric verses the humiliation of the peasants. His "muse of vengeance" represented his desire for vengeance on the oppressors of the serfs and peasants. But only in his verses was he able to identify with their lot. His own life was spent in the manner of a gentleman. Since he was unable to identify himself completely with those whom he pitied and wished to redeem, he suffered from a split between belief and action, and from an inconsistency between conviction and way of life. This resulted in self-reproach and self-condemnation. Nekrasov was never to forget the plight of the peasants nor to cease to think with contrition of the fact that he as a gentleman lived better than they and was born to higher status. This contrast in fate and fortune is the refrain of his mature verse and the recurring theme of his "penitent poems." Nekrasov and members of his school indulged in self-reproach because they felt themselves cut off from the *narod* (the "common people," the "masses," the "nation") and at the same time had renounced their own class. They despaired of reaching the *narod* with their message while regretting that their words were not transformed into deeds and that they did not take active part in the reshaping of society which they preached. They accused themselves alone, however, and not others or society in general, and therein lies a great difference from the writers with the widely popular theme of the "superfluous man," so well-known from the works of Turgenev and Goncharov.

I *Serfdom and the Great Reform*

For the American reader the term "serf" can be misleading. The institution of serfdom, as it existed in Russia for many centuries, naturally underwent many changes, but at no time did it correspond exactly to the forms of slavery that existed in the south of the United States. The dictionary defines a serf as a person whose service is attached to the soil and transferred with it. In the course of time, Russia developed its own special forms of the institution, so that comparisons with the serfdom of medieval Western Europe must be made with qualifications. The growth of serfdom in Russia is intimately associated with the development of strong central government in the principality of Muscovy. Large amounts of land, a relatively thin peasant population, and the increasing need of the state for soldiers and administrators forced successive grand princes and later czars to grant populated lands to military retainers and then promulgate laws reducing and eventually (1649) completely destroying the mobility of the peasants entering into voluntary serfdom in return for loans or other forms of aid. Most voluntary serfs came from among the so-called black peasants—freeholders who owed allegiance and taxes to the czar and were simply transferred together with their land to the rising class of *pomeshchiki.* Serfs who migrated to the city usually continued to pay *obrok,* a payment in lieu of service in the fields or household.

Russia also knew slavery from the earliest times. Slaves were officially recognized by law until 1649. The czars did not care for slavery because slaves were free from military service and taxes; serfs, nominally men and not chattels, were subject to both. Slavery and serfdom did not merge in any strict sense; they existed as parallel institutions until the former was abolished. As the central government gradually surrendered its administrative and judicial control over the serfs, a process completed by the eighteenth century, the life of serfs came to resemble that of slaves. Serfs were sold apart from land and often apart from their families. They were sold through the classified advertisements in the St. Petersburg newspapers. Ironically, the serf's liability for taxes made him a man rather than a slave. The law of 1762, which freed the nobility from compulsory state service, but which did nothing to change the nobles' grip on the serfs, is an interesting turning point in the development of the institution.

Among educated Russians there were very different attitudes toward serfdom. The conservative gentry approved of serfdom and autocracy. They resisted the idea of abolition until Alexander II, in 1857, decreed that serfdom must end. The Slavophils opposed serfdom but approved of autocracy. They wanted to free the peasants from the degrading control of the gentry. They wished the peasants to be organized economically and administratively on the basis of the primordial peasant community—the *mir*. The liberals were opposed to serfdom and ultimately to autocracy. But—and here an inner inconsistency begins—they believed that in the conditions of the 1850's and 1860's only an autocrat could do away with serfdom. Therefore they accepted as compromises during the period of the emancipation institutions which ultimately undermined their own hope for constitutionalism. The radicals were against both serfdom and autocracy. They sought a socialist solution to the serf problem, placing their hopes on the peasant *mir* as a basis for a rapid transition to socialism. The reforms which we mention in the next paragraph were carried out with the support of the liberals and against the opposition of both the radicals and the conservatives.

When Alexander II came to the throne after the death of Nicholas I in February, 1855, great hopes were entertained by many of the intelligentsia for a new era in Russian life. Czar Alexander set out almost immediately to initiate what is called the "age of the Great Reforms." Planning for the Emancipation of 1861 began shortly after Alexander's accession to the throne. The actual emancipation was accompanied by the introduction of peasant local self-government in the form of village communes (*sel'skoe obshchestvo*) and township administrations (*volost'*). In 1864 the *zemstvo* was introduced, meaning self-government for all classes. This operated at two levels, namely the district (*uyezd*) and province (*gubernia*). Judicial reform, including trial by jury, was introduced in 1864. A reform in the structure of municipal government took place in 1870. The universities were given at least nominal autonomy in 1863, although student meetings and publications were still strictly controlled; police surveillance was routine at times of trouble.

Western historians do not usually question the sincerity and value of these reforms. Earlier Soviet historians and critics, on the other hand, liked to point out that many of the reforms were but window-dressing and that in back of them stood an unregenerate government with an active and ubiquitous secret police, a widespread system of informers and agents, and a civil service that was overstaffed, underpaid, and only moderately intelligent. Worst of all, the most important reform, the emancipation of the serfs, proceeded in such a way that the peasants were loaded with new debts and saddled with extended litigation over procurement of the land. More recent Soviet scholarship on the Great Reforms concedes that they were "progressive," that is, they prepared the basis for and made possible the development of capital and industry in Russia. However it may be seen by historians, the peasants were so bitterly disappointed by the terms of the emancipation that large numbers of them rebelled.

It may have been impossible in any case to achieve an equitable redistribution of the land after so many years and in view of the number of people involved. But the contractual basis which the government committee arrived at created maximum confusion and invited endless lawsuits or alternatively crushing payments. The government compensated the landlords for the land which they surrendered to the peasants; this was done on a contract basis, with two years allowed for the landlords to reach agreement with the peasants. The redemption prices paid by the government were set somewhat above the current market value of the land. The price arrived at in the settlement with the government was to serve as the basis for purchase of the land by the former serfs. Not until 1883 was a state-owned land bank established; the purpose of this bank was to assist peasants in acquiring their property. Thus for over twenty years the so-called redemption payments, the fixed annual sums paid by the peasants for the land which they received out of landlords' estates, had to be earned by whatever means they could find or invent. The redemption payments, originally scheduled to spread over forty-nine years, were postponed for a time in the 1890's and finally canceled in 1906.[2] But by this time the damage was done.

Long after the reform, the memory of serfdom and, as we have indicated, the financial burdens on the ex-serfs, continued and influenced the steady growth of radical thinking among both the intelligentsia and the peasants. The resulting problems never came to rest within the lifetime of Nekrasov. Since the statutes of 1849 there had always been peasant revolts. During the period of

1826 to 1854 there were 712 revolts which the government officially admitted; 348 of these took place between 1845 and 1854. The reader must not forget that this social unrest forms the background for Nekrasov's poems. The Crimean War, 1853–56, impoverished the country and disturbed peasant life with extra force because of the increased recruitment for the army. The war raised the peasants' hopes and intensified their restlessness. Simultaneously the revelation of Russia's backwardness and conflict with the Western powers and their superior technology contributed directly and vitally to the period of the great reforms. On the eve of the Emancipation there were twenty-two and one-half million serfs in European Russia out of an estimated total population of sixty million.

When Nekrasov speaks of the *narod*, he often means not only serfs in the strict sense, but also free peasants and commoners, in fact everyone but the privileged and the aristocracy. As used by Nekrasov, the word usually has a special, polemic quality. The poet was also a contemporary of the first real wave of urbanization, a process that produced the urban proletariat and the growing class of artisans and other *raznochintsy*, many of whom were becoming both literate and vocal by the 1840's. Both Belinsky and Dostoyevsky, for example, were *raznochintsy*. In 1812 about 4½ per cent of the population lived in cities; by the middle of the century the figure had risen to about 8 per cent. Nekrasov also lived through the first period of industrialization and the development of early capitalism. The technological advances of the time find few echoes in his poetry, but the suffering and the dislocation of peasants attendant upon them provide him with his most persistent themes.

Serfdom and its evils; a corrupt and octopuslike bureaucracy, which among other things enforced a total and stupid censorship; political repression which stifled all initiative; excessive leisure and license on the part of the often only semiliterate gentry—these were the conditions of life which the young Nekrasov found about him. The energy of his best years was spent in conflict with them. Russia was a land of feudal darkness, divided sharply into oppressors and oppressed. Many of the intelligentsia were educated abroad and were consequently aware of Russia's backwardness. But the intelligentsia was dependent on the agrarian serf-economy and was conscious of the difficulties of changing anything. Although its members frequently harbored liberal and critical opinions, they in fact feared loss of privilege through reform almost as much as the autocratic regime on which they felt they depended. The result was reconciliation with things as they were, resignation, and a growing sense of futility and superfluousness. Nekrasov, torn between his heritage and his true sympathies, was not spared these feelings. In his journalistic writings and in his poems he tried to make a specific contribution and to palliate his conscience. But as he himself emphasized, such activity was only verbal, so that he too suffered from that sense of discrepancy between belief and action which is so characteristic of the intelligentsia of the early nineteenth century.

The effectiveness of much of his writing derives from this tension. Toward himself and his country he had an attitude of love-hate. The final words of his poem on the death of the admired Gogol are: "How he loved—hating!" (I, 65). This note is sounded several times in his poetry: "He who lives without grief and anger/Does not love his fatherland" (II, 222). And: "That heart will not learn to love/Which has grown weary of hating" (I, 158). Nevertheless, the dominant note of his poetry remains the basic affection which clearly underlies both his aggressive satire and his sorrow. He always affirmed the dual nature of his muse of vengeance and grief, but the feeling of genuine love for Russia and for Russian people is communicated in most of his poems. At the same time, there is an element of social criticism even in his most intimate and confessional lyrics, and it is this combination of themes that gives him his individual stamp.

The span of Nekrasov's life embraces the great developments of the mid-century and accompanies the profound and epoch-making changes such as the Peasant Reform (1861) that took place in the political and economic sphere as well as in literature. He made his literary debut at a time when a new reading public was appearing. It was for the commoners, the *raznochintsy*, that Nekrasov founded his monthly magazine *The Contemporary* in 1847. The landed gentry was suffering increasingly from a sense of futility and frustration, for it was becoming more and more aware of its obsolescence, its lack of purpose and proper function in society. The process by which the gentry lost its social, political, and economic leadership possibilities was accompanied by its decline in intellectual leadership. The 1850's were the years of transition to the "age of the commoner." As this process of change continued it gathered speed, so that in the 1860's and 1870's the leaders were no longer the "men of the '40's" but the new generation of radical revolutionaries.

II *Nekrasov and the Radicals*

Nekrasov did more than merely keep in step with these shifts and changes. He was from the beginning of his career in the vanguard and was often the leader and spokesman of the radical intelligentsia. In the 1840's he was a vigorous propagandist for the "natural school," that is, the realism founded on the contemporary understanding of Gogol. He continued the tradition of popular poetry established by Koltsov, but added his own note of social criticism. He gathered about him the most influential critics of his time. An older generation of literary historians even considered Nekrasov's greatest contribution to Russian intellectual life to be his fostering of the great critics: Belinsky in the 1840's, Chernyshevsky and Dobroliubov in the 1850's. Many active revolutionaries were contributors to *The Contemporary*. In the 1860's the real revolutionaries looked to that periodical as their ideological guide. With some justice Turgenev called Chernyshevsky and Dobroliubov "literary Robespierres" . . . when he did not refer to them as "snake and rattlesnake." In the 1870's many Populists who "went to the people" did so because of the inspiration of Nekrasov's verses. It is no exaggeration to say the youth of the day learned of the condition of the *narod* from the immensely popular poetry of Nekrasov.

Nekrasov's leadership in radical revolutionary criticism, his biting satire, and his emphasis on vengeance and grief should be taken as manifestations of his love for Russia, not as many conservatives and Slavophils would have it as disloyalty to his country and his people. "Love for one's fatherland means above all the deep, passionate and fruitful wish for its good and its enlightenment, the readiness to devote to it one's possessions and one's very life, the passionate sympathy for all that is good in it and the noble discontent with that which obstructs its path to perfection" (IX, 301). Obviously the element of social criticism in Nekrasov's writings has not escaped the notice of Soviet critics, about half of whose comments on the poet might be summarized in the oft-quoted statement that he loved the *narod* and hated its oppressors. They have found much material to document their claims, for Nekrasov was quite frank about his tendentiousness. He did not believe in "pure poetry" remote from man's problems here and now. "There is no science for science's sake, no art for art's sake—they all exist in society, for the improvement of man, for his enrichment in knowledge and the material needs of life" (IX, 296).

Nekrasov was a materialist, probably also an atheist, who believed in progress through enlightenment and the betterment of living conditions. Such a philosophy of life is sufficient to make him the darling of the Soviets, but it is not the only aspect which interests a modern reader. Nekrasov's dual nature is expressed in most of his human relations as well as in his writing. He loved his mother and sympathized with her hard lot in life while hating and rejecting his father. He loved but quarreled with Avdotia Panayeva. He felt called to write, but despised himself for not doing more. His relations to friends like Turgenev, Annenkov, and Botkin, with whom he collaborated for years, also reflect his tendency toward love-hate. As far as can be reconstructed from the available evidence, this split in his sensibility goes back to the impressions of violent contrasts of his childhood. It was strengthened during his early days in St. Petersburg, when for years he suffered from hunger and deprivation, spending his nights in flophouses and his days writing and starving.

Thus there came to be two N. A. Nekrasovs, a poet with a poet's sensitivity and flights of imagination, and a hardheaded businessman, capable of successful journalistic enterprise, full of managerial competence, a gambler at the elite English Club and friend of noblemen, but also a hunter who spent weeks with peasant hunting guides listening to their stories and songs. The testimony of his friends in St. Petersburg confirms the impression of the dual nature of the poet. Those who knew him only as a man of letters at the teas and receptions so charmingly presided over by Madame Panayeva commented with astonishment on his business acumen as editor and publisher, wondered at his long evenings playing cards at the English Club, and were mostly unaware of his frequent escapes to the country to hunt in the company of peasants.

He was unprepossessing in appearance, and spoke diffidently with a high, squeaky voice. When he read poems to a group, it was usually necessary to dissociate the person reading from the poem being read, in order to appreciate the quality of the verse.

Nekrasov made no secret of his radical views and of his sympathy with the oppressed and downtrodden, but he maintained cordial relations with members of the gentry and nobility, sought favor with the censors, and moved in the "better" social circles that he often castigated in satire. It is small wonder then that the habit grew up among his friends and acquaintances of distinguishing the man from the poetry. Since he valued the principles of his friends and co-workers more highly than the sentimental ties of friendship, it is not surprising that he quarreled with Dostoyevsky, whom he lampooned in scurrilous epigrams; with Turgenev, of whom for years he was an intimate friend, and with Tolstoy, to whom for a long period he wrote solicitous and pleading letters. These three great writers seemed to Nekrasov to be too liberal, that is, to be reconciled to the status quo. By 1860 all members of the group that had once gathered around Belinsky—Botkin, Druzhinin, Annenkov, and Turgenev—had broken with him and *The Contemporary.* Dobroliubov was loyal to him until his death, and Chernyshevsky also remained faithful to him; but after his exile, Nekrasov was again alone and without close human relationships. Except for the years with Avdotia Panayeva, with whom his relations were difficult and often embittering, and a few years with Dobroliubov and Chernyshevsky, Nekrasov was a lonely, solitary man, conscious of his isolation and suffering from it. For much of his life he was starved for companionship, friendship, and understanding.

Nekrasov entered the literary world just after the death of Pushkin (1837) and shortly before the death of Lermontov (1841). With the departure of these two most famous Russian poets, a period of decline in verse set in. Many literary historians refer to the period as an age of prose. It was an age of epigones in verse, of pseudo-Romanticism and imitation. Nekrasov's first publication, the adolescent poems *Dreams and Sounds,* whose very title betrays its Romantic nature, shows nowhere the hand of the master. Instead it seems like an epitaph to the great age of poetry.

In the mid 1840's Belinsky declared authoritatively that an age of prose had begun and that prose was the only proper medium for the tasks of the 1840's. The works of Gogol seemed to prove his point. Belinsky's adverse review of Nekrasov's youthful verses combined a repetition of his views on the necessity of prose with an attack on pseudopoetry and the vapid limitations of Pushkin's Romantic phase.

III *Belinsky*

The real Nekrasov, the Nekrasov of the unmistakable stamp and tone, came into being only after his contact with Belinsky. Since we are concerned only with the mature and awakened Nekrasov, it is important for us to know about this great and enduring influence on the poet, this incomparable critic who awakened the poet from his Romantic dreams. Vissarion G. Belinsky is one of the most fascinating and important figures of the 1840's. Few men as literary critics have ever influenced literature so dramatically. In an age when literature was all-important, and was in spite of censorship the only real outlet for the intellectual energies of the period, Belinsky exercised for years a domination in the field of letters that is unparalleled. The Belinsky whom Nekrasov came to know toward the end of 1841 had overcome a phase of speculative philosophy and had turned all his fierce energies to social criticism. With zeal and dedication he set out to attack the appalling evils of Russian civilization: the ignorance and squalor of the serfs, the ignorance and hypocritical conformance to the status quo of the clergy; the ignorance, brutality, and mendacity of the upper classes; the ignorance and grasping greed of the merchants—in sum the whole backward, corrupt, and benighted way of life in which Russia was bogged down.

In an age when literature was the only vehicle by which political and social ideas could be conveyed, Belinsky became the czar of letters through the ardor of his convictions and the fervor of his principles. In literary criticism he had two main targets of attack: the derivative literature that slavishly imitated French or other foreign models, and the uncritically idealizing folklore and local-color nationalism of the Romantic epigones. He believed that realistic description of Russian social conditions, if achieved with artistic imagination, would of itself help to mobilize the reading public against the regime. Since he has been idolized by the Soviets, it is good to recall that although widely read, he was only half-educated. His prose style was often labored and prolix, his lines of thought frequently tortuous; but the moral force and the power of his personality carried conviction. Regarding whatever he believed in he remained uncompromising and incorruptible. People as different in temperament and judgment as Herzen and Turgenev, Annenkov and Ogarëv, Dostoyevsky and Nekrasov himself all agreed that he was the moral guide and preceptor of the intelligentsia of the 1840's. His revolt against the barbarous stagnation of Russian intellectual life inspired a whole generation of writers. All the later radical revolutionaries claimed descent from him and even some liberals came for a time under his spell.

For Nekrasov, the meeting with Belinsky was the turning point of his life. All that had gone before was renounced as a prelude; all that was to come bore the stamp of Belinsky's influence. The transformation of the young poet was so swift and so complete, we must conclude that Nekrasov's inner development had reached a point of readiness and receptivity for the new revelation. In their relationship was a remarkable case of spiritual affinity. The poet's personal life was changed too, for it was Belinsky who introduced him to the Panayevs. After the adverse criticism of *Dreams and Sounds,* it was Nekrasov's early reviews which attracted Belinsky's attention. Their critical views seemed to bear great similarity in attitude. Soon their critical reviews, written independently, sounded so much alike that it was possible for the reading public to be confused as to the true authorship. Nekrasov's hardships in the lower depths of St. Petersburg had brought him to grips with "reality"; but "realism" in the literary sense is not just the description of reality: it is reality seen through the prism of a creative imagination. Personal experiences of hardship are not sufficient to supply a poet with the power to depict life; therefore some inner change, which we can only assume to have existed, must have been completed within Nekrasov in the years 1841–42.

However we conceive of the influence of Belinsky on Nekrasov —from the early 1840's on—poet and critic agree that art must be an expression of the national condition, that the artist must represent the truth as he sees it, and that social and moral considerations are higher than political or esthetic ones. Whether this viewpoint be the heritage of Belinsky, or the personal achievement of Nekrasov, or some combination of the two is not so important as the fact that Nekrasov remained true to the principles of the 1840's throughout his life. Of all those who gathered about Belinsky in St. Petersburg in the 1840's, Nekrasov alone consistently upheld during the difficult years that followed the ideals enunciated by Belinsky.

We cannot emphasize often enough that in this period literature was the only outlet for the creative imagination and the sole form of intellectual expression available to the intelligentsia. The 1840's saw the first triumphs of the literary movement known as Realism. As has been suggested already, this Realism rests on the contemporary interpretation of Gogol's work. To the modern reader the element of the fantastic, the irrational, and the absurd is the most striking thing about his work. But when his *Dead Souls* appeared in 1842 it was hailed as a masterpiece of Realism. Gogol was praised as a satirical Realist who had brilliantly portrayed the social realities of contemporary Russia. In the 1850's Chernyshevsky referred to the period as the "Age of Gogol." Unfortunately, Soviet critics have reverted to the Belinsky-Chernyshevsky view of Gogol as a satirical Social Realist, and they tend to see the playfully fantastic in him as secondary to his social criticism. But it is true that Gogol did deal directly with the contemporary national scene, and that in itself is sufficient to satisfy a basic tenet of the Realism propounded by Belinsky and his circle. Nekrasov seemed to have a special affinity for Gogol, finding in him traits of his own and ascribing to him attitudes and positions which Nekrasov felt especially congenial. He praised Gogol for his lyricism, his subjectivity, and his very personal reactions to the reality about him.[3] It was the common battle for the "Gogol tendency" in literature which brought Belinsky and Nekrasov together and gave them a common cause for which to fight, for Gogol's approach to Russian reality was the ideal held up by Belinsky. From Gogol Nekrasov learned how to treat contemporary, local themes,[4] thereby completing the transition from his dreamy Romanticism to his firm and critical treatment of the social and political problems of his day. Nekrasov discovered his true nature and calling through personal contacts with Belinsky and literary contact with Gogol. Throughout his life he continued to grow and develop as poet and writer, but the direction of the growth was determined by Belinsky.

CHAPTER 2

The Beginnings in Criticism, Jingles, and Journalism

ALTHOUGH Nekrasov had not done well at the Gymnasium in Yaroslavl', his first thought on going to St. Petersburg in 1838 was to enter the university there. His father had sent him to the capital to enter the army, and upon hearing of his failure to attend regimental school cut him off from all financial support. For the next three years Nekrasov led the life of a pauper, quite literally penniless, often begging in order to prevent starvation, taking any small jobs that he could, but still determined to become a man of letters. After several attempts to pass the examinations for the university, all of which ended in failure, he gave up his plans for further formal education and devoted his energies to writing. During these first few years in St. Petersburg he produced an enormous amount of material, most of it ephemeral and trivial. He wrote and wrote: comedies, both original and translations; vaudeville skits; reviews and essays; in short, anything that might be published. The sentimental, imitative, and Romantic *Dreams and Sounds* failed to sell at all. The book did, however, attract the unfavorable attention of the critics, notably Belinsky, but that did not discourage Nekrasov, who continued his attempts to make his way as a writer.

As early as 1838 the poet had succeeded in having some of his poems printed, mostly in the periodicals *Son of the Fatherland* and *Reading Library*. But his first important breakthrough came when he became a contributor to F. A. Koni's *Pantheon of the Russian and all European Theaters* in 1840. During his first experience in journalism he gained valuable practice, and through Koni he came into contact with some of the literary circles in St. Petersburg. Belinsky, it should be noted, viewed the *Pantheon* favorably at this time. In 1840 Nekrasov also became a contributor of reviews and articles to Koni's *Literary Gazette*. This position gave him access to contacts with both writers and publishers, among them Krayevsky, the publisher of *Notes of the Fatherland*, the periodical that was then Belinsky's chief forum. Nekrasov's contributions to which publication were mainly prose after the failure of his volume of verse. Years later in an autobiographical fragment (XII, 23), the poet spoke of his turn to prose as a turn to the truth. Most of his early prose tales were published under a pseudonym. They were quite frankly written "for bread," and have no literary value, as Nekrasov readily admitted in the above-mentioned reference. But their themes do illustrate some of Nekrasov's enduring concerns and anticipate his later works in verse. He gradually learned to give up exotic subjects of which he had had no first-hand observation and turned to his own experiences: he wrote of young writers who failed in the capital, of the power of money, of fallen women, of usurers and hypocritical officials—all topics which concerned him for many years afterward.

More important are the skits, playlets, and vaudevilles done for the theater. In the 1840's the theater played an important role in the public and intellectual life of St. Petersburg. The theater was one of the few public institutions open to all levels of society. The czar and his court attended the Alexander Theater, but so did any commoners who could afford it. It hardly needs to be mentioned that the theater was under the strict control and surveillance of the government and government censorship.

In general two types of drama were favored: historical plays of great bombast and strong monarchistic slant, and vaudevilles and farces which were meant to entertain and distract. Much of what Nekrasov submitted to the theater consisted of either translations from the French or of adaptations of foreign originals. Yet even in these early, rather trivial works he was able to introduce some social criticism in his favorite themes of the uneducated landowner, the corrupt bureaucrat who takes bribes, and the usurer who bleeds his victims.[1] Most of Nekrasov's vaudevilles were produced during 1841 and 1842, but only in 1841 did he write original ones. Once again in 1844 he wrote "A Usurer of St. Petersburg," an original vaudeville in rhymed couplets. "The Actor," written in 1841, is probably his most successful piece for the stage. The general level of his production was about the same as that of his contemporaries. When not practicing his dactylic rhymes he resorted to trivial puns. The following is an example of his trivial play on words: "I'm on my knees before you,/Put me back on my feet!" (IV, 67). The poet did not take this sort of thing seriously and even made fun of his own tendency to pun.[2]

One of Nekrasov's earliest satires is his verse *feuilleton* "A Provincial Scribe." It is the first of a series of satires in verse, more humorous than severely critical, and characteristic only for his early works in this vein. In later years his satire became much sharper and more biting. It is written in couplets with three-foot iambs; the rhymes are alternately dactylic and masculine. The versification is quite mechanical and repetitious, and the hand of the master is not yet evident. It appeared in three sections of the magazine *Pantheon of the Russian and all European Theaters* in 1840. Each chapter is a separate *feuilleton,* and each successive one is but a loose continuation of the preceding one. Nekrasov also used this rather undemanding form later in "The Chatterbox," 1843. Since he was writing in a magazine for the theater, Nekrasov included "reviews" of current plays at the Alexander Theater. But these are hardly serious reviews, and critical evaluation is scarcely evident since their main purpose is to give the comic responses of a rustic. The fictional character, through whose eyes the theater and the life of the capital are seen, is called Feoklit Onufrich Bob; he is a provincial bumpkin, a minor official of the type common in the vaudeville plays of the time, obsequious, bribe-taking, mildly amusing in his bewilderment. There is nothing original here, and nothing that would suggest the future poet except a certain glibness in versification. Unfortunately these satiric verses are characteristic of Nekrasov's production for the first few years of the 1840's.

In spite of the occasional successful satiric thrusts, the literary value of these skits and farces is not high. But they were a valuable training ground for the poet. He developed facility in the rhymed vaudeville couplet, skill in wordplay and in the Aesopian language necessary to elude the censors. Some of his skits were quite successful and were well received by the critics and the public. In any case they form an interesting period in his rapid growth as a writer, for they mark the transition from his early Romanticism to an ever increasing control of the techniques of realism. St. Petersburg and its daily life and problems came more and more to supply the topics for both his prose and his satiric verse.

I *Early Criticism*

Side by side with the training in versification and in the treatment of topical themes, Nekrasov developed an increasingly sharp critical judgment. Perhaps he had already taken to heart Pushkin's dictum that the state of criticism is by itself an indication of the degree of development which a literature has attained. Since it was his achievements as a critic rather than as a poet that attracted Belinsky to him, we must recall that Nekrasov had on his own initiative become an astute critic and sound judge of literature before he became acquainted with Belinsky. Even while his own production was either trivial or still tuned to Romanticism he had started to parody other Romantic epigones. It would appear that his development as a critic preceded his maturity as a creative writer. Nekrasov seemed instinctively to share Belinsky's view that the influence of criticism is not so much on art or the creation of art as on the taste and judgment of the public. He set out to educate the public at a time when his own original works lagged far behind his critical standards. Nekrasov was never an abstract thinker nor in any way a speculative philosopher, and thus was by nature predisposed to agree with Belinsky's thesis that criticism rested as much on a social and political foundation as it did on analysis of literary form. By 1842 both the poet and the critic had developed a theory of the interaction of criticism and literature, and both were convinced of the primacy of a social purpose in all forms of writing.

Nekrasov was instinctively drawn to satire and parody rather than to analytic prose in essay form. Even his earliest reviews and critical articles already displayed an individual and characteristic technique. He often proceeded by quoting carefully selected lush passages and interpolating them in his own sober prose. Or he retold a story, but in his own way, showing up by the form of his retelling the ridiculous aspects of the story under review.[3] He was very adept at rendering ridiculous the targets of his criticism. To an unusual degree he possessed a keen sense for the ludicrous, the strained or artificial.

In all, Nekrasov wrote about one hundred pieces of criticism.

His first reviews appeared in 1841 in Koni's *Pantheon*. It was, as he humorously wrote later, a period of learning by doing.[4] His chief parodistic thrusts were directed at the trivial writers of entertainment literature and at the epigones of Romanticism. Common to both these groups was a tendency to avoid the reality around them and find their themes in mythology or remote history.[5] Bulgarin's reactionary, feudalistic pseudonationalism was a favorite target. The idyllic school that represented rustic life in glowing terms came under vicious attack for its distortion of the truth. As a theater critic, Nekrasov polemicized against the poverty of ideas in the contemporary theater. He especially deplored the lack of plays dealing with topical themes and displaying a broad, socially oriented grip on reality.[6] By the mid 1840's, when he had reached maturity as a critic, he increased his demands for a sober and just view of reality—that is, all reality—and particularly the dark side of contemporary life.

Much of his activity as a critic was devoted to fostering popular themes in literature and descriptions of actual life as lived by the *narod*. But he sternly opposed a false Naturalism which contented itself with a mere registering of the facts: he called upon writers to confess openly their position, views, and sympathies and to participate actively in the formation of the thought and views of the world. Since he considered the esthetic value of literature to be inseparable from the ideas expressed, he often started his critique by examining the basic ideas of the writers concerned.[7] He became so much like Belinsky in style and method that one of his programmatic reviews in 1847 was long ascribed to Belinsky.[8]

One of Nekrasov's most influential articles was his "Russian Poets of the Second Rank," 1849. This article was a major contribution to the criticism of the time. Nekrasov was the first to point out the importance and excellence of the neglected poet Tiutchev. It is not too much to say that Nekrasov rescued him from near oblivion. Tiutchev's power to evoke nature was given special praise (IX, 205). His connection with the heritage of his great predecessors, Pushkin and Lermontov, was first established in this article. The characteristic quality of Tiutchev's verse with its gentle irony received its first appreciation at the hand of Nekrasov. Tiutchev, who had ceased to write, was greatly encouraged and renewed his literary efforts. Nekrasov had the courage to predict an important place in literature for this poet who was hardly known to the public, and he took pleasure in seeing his prophecy fulfilled.

Belinsky's dictum that prose had replaced verse in the 1840's and that prose was the only adequate means for the further development of Realism was accepted only with reservations by Nekrasov, who saw the dangers in the neglect of poetry and the possibility of a break in tradition and the accompanying loss of acquired competence in verse. He shared the great critic's view that the decay of poetry was a result of the narrowness of its themes and its remoteness from contemporary reality. He observed the use of outworn language, most of it inherited from Pushkin or Lermontov, and the undue emphasis on smoothness of language and perfection of form to the neglect of content. His first concern, then, as a critic, was to call for a renewal of subject matter and ideas.[9] The theorists of "pure poetry," who considered themselves the heirs of Pushkin (as opposed to Gogol), among them A. V. Druzhinin, S. S. Dudyshkin, and P. V. Annenkov, treated Nekrasov's opinions on poetry with disdain. In his presence they usually dissimulated their contempt, but in letters to each other they scoffed at his theories. They continued to collaborate with the great editor of the leading periodical of the time, but during the dark years from the death of Belinsky to the coming of Chernyshevsky, Nekrasov was alone and lonely.

His crowning work as a critic is represented by a series of articles written from 1855 to 1856 in collaboration with Chernyshevsky. These "Notes on Periodicals" are his last sustained effort as a critic. Nekrasov was well aware that he did not formulate his esthetic views with the same systematic clarity and incisiveness characteristic of Chernyshevsky and Dobroliubov. For long periods of time, he turned from criticism in formal essays, leaving this task to the critics whom he fostered, and expressed his views in satirical verse—which replaced his prose reviews and articles. In his final effort as critic he continued along the lines of his earlier essays, defending the Realism of Gogol, championing the plays of Ostrovsky, and seeking to elucidate the true nature of Pushkin's heritage. He defended Pushkin against those who wished to make him the standard-bearer of "pure poetry" by pointing out the critical Realism to be found in Pushkin's later works.[10] Realism which depicted life as it was did not suffice: a note of protest was necessary, for one must point out the tasks to be done, the promise for the future, and the necessity for action. As an advocate of Realism of this kind Nekrasov not only interpreted Pushkin very differently from most of his contemporaries, but was also able to see important aspects of such works of Turgenev as his *Sportsman's Notes* and *Rudin.*[11]

Turgenev's *Rudin* needed defense not only from the attacks of the conservatives, who considered it a failure, but also from the harsh views of Nekrasov's close friends and colleagues, Chernyshevsky and Dobroliubov. Nekrasov was more tolerant of the "superfluous man" than they were, tended more to see the historical necessity of the type, and affirmed in his poem "Sasha": "He sows good seed nonetheless" (I, 128). Nekrasov understood Rudin as representing the best of the society of the 1840's and as a quite natural product of the historical conditions. His own Aragin of the poem "Sasha," published at nearly the same time, was portrayed as a contemporary hero, that is, a figure of the 1850's, and therefore the poet drew him as a poseur and empty phrase-maker. Nekrasov considered historical accuracy very important, just as necessary for the understanding of a work such as *Rudin* as the portrayal of the social level of the characters. He admired Turgenev's precision of language and his method of characterizing the person speaking by the level of language assigned to him. But he also wished there to be perfect clarity concerning the location in history of the types portrayed by the great novelist.

II *First Publications*

Nekrasov's own style in his critical writings was often conversational and chatty. It was less logical and theoretical than Belinsky's, less aggressive and incisive than Chernyshevsky's. It was not based on erudition—Nekrasov had little formal education—but it attempted to create a dialogue between reader and critic. At times he openly invited the reader to share in the experience: "Come, dear reader, and give me your hand, and we shall get along peacefully together, and converse openly with one another" (IX, 453). The invitation to dialogue lent charm and intimacy to many of his reviews. There was both humility and firmness of purpose in his addresses to his readers: "Teach us to be better than we are; plant in us respect for the good and the beautiful, do not tolerate society's fashionable apathy towards dubious or despicable conditions, but expose and pursue such conditions in the name of truth, conscience, and human dignity; explain to us our obligations as human beings and as citizens—we still understand them with so little clarity" (IX, 291). His critical activity was important for his own growth and was influential in shaping the views of his contemporaries, but we must note that criticism was but a small part of his creative life and was confined to short and intermittent periods of effort. When he had achieved assurance and mastery as a poet, he fell silent as a critic.

In 1843 Nekrasov undertook to publish for the first time. In February he published an almanac entitled *Articles in Verse Without Pictures*, with contributions from other authors as well as a verse *feuilleton* of his own. In June he was able to publish a second issue, and with this modest success he began his career as publisher and editor. There is little to distinguish the almanac from other almanacs of that day and age since humorous verses were the usual content of such publications. There was some contemporary satire, and various descriptions of life in St. Petersburg were presented, but nothing that rose conspicuously above the contemporary level. Nekrasov's contribution consisted of "The Chatterer," a fictitious character created for satiric purposes, behind whose mask the poet indulged in ironic praise of the regime. In the figure of the chatterbox he gave a portrait of a petty official and his many weaknesses and prejudices, his corrupt but stylish way of living, and his dubious means of getting ahead in the capital. Each section starts with the petty official describing himself; then follow loosely linked impressions of various entertainments and distractions in St. Petersburg: books, theatrical and church ceremonies, concerts, and the like. It is written in comic dactylic rhymes, and with many puns of little subtlety. The obsequious attitude toward the nobility and toward titles, the prevalence of bribe-taking, and the struggle for advancement and status are some of the objects of the satire. Much in this rhymed satire coincides with Nekrasov's reviews.

For the first time Nekrasov proved himself equal to a large responsibility with his second almanac, *The Physiology of St. Petersburg*, prepared during 1844 but not passed by the censors until

1845.[12] He performed his task as editor with great skill. The almanac was not only a financial success but also a splendid first manifesto for the "natural school," Belinsky's term for the Realism based on Gogol. A "physiological sketch" meant at that time a description of reality in all its observable aspects, but it meant especially a description of the dark and seamy sides of life with special attention to the lower classes, combined with a satirical view of the upper classes. The programmatic introductory article was written by Belinsky, whose total of four articles took up more than a third of the two volumes. Nekrasov's contributions consisted of the prose "The Corners of St. Petersburg," a series of vignettes of life in the lower depths of the capital, and the poem "The Bureaucrat." The fictitious hero of this satiric poem is very similar to that of "The Chatterer"; he is a successful bribe-taker, a favorite target of the "natural school." He is also a passionate theatergoer, thereby offering the author an opportunity to satirize both the theater and the public's generally bad taste. There were in the poem several echoes of Belinsky, but the basic theme, that of hypocrisy, is a new note in Nekrasov. The irony seems today rather heavy and obvious, but the work won high praise from Belinsky. Nekrasov's prose contribution contains some Gogolian exaggeration in the description of the people of the corners of St. Petersburg, and in general there are many echoes of Gogol and his techniques. Nekrasov made much use of proverbs, folk sayings, popular speech forms, and mannerisms of speech in order to characterize his subjects; but he avoided both vulgarisms and regionalisms in language. He succeeded in drawing his characters with sympathy, but without sentimentality. In portraying people who were down and out, he was not content merely to describe their wretched condition, but tried to show the causes for their failure in life.

One of Nekrasov's last verse *feuilletons* in this period is the poem "The News," 1845. It was chiefly a satire on the new dance fad of the time, the polka. In this work the poet did not create a fictitious hero as his mouthpiece, but spoke in his own voice. Modish forms of dress, social climbing, status seeking, and the general triviality and mindlessness of society life furnished targets for his satiric thrusts. Nekrasov's humor in this as in other, similar works during the 1840's often took the form of hyperbole. Many of his exaggerations lack subtlety: a young man who commits suicide when he is not promoted; another youth who grows melancholy and fades away when a supposedly rich bride turns out to be poor. Much better is the implied lesson in the newspaper announcement that depicts side by side and without commentary a stray dog and a governess who has run away. The language of this jingle, like that of its predecessor "The Bureaucrat," is full of prose turns of speech, many of them deliberately derived from bureaucratic jargon, with inversions and stiff formulas. The five-foot iambs give an amusing turn to the prose clichés and emphasize the imitative nature of the language while increasing its comic effect. In "The News" there are also several echoes of Pushkin as well as other parodistic quotations and allusions. But the irony is not directed at Pushkin, rather it is aimed at the idle use of poetic embellishment. The intent, as in his later parodies of Lermontov, was not to make fun of a great poet but to counterattack the epigones of Romantic high style with their own exoticisms and affections.

The third almanac published by Nekrasov, *An Anthology of St. Petersburg,* was a literary triumph. For the first time Nekrasov succeeded in gathering a group which represented brilliantly the new Gogol school. Contributors were Belinsky, Herzen, Turgenev, Dostoyevsky, Odoyevsky, I. I. Panayev, Nekrasov himself, and Maikov. In addition there were translations of Shakespeare, Goethe, and Byron. Fortunately it was a financial success, for according to Madame Panayeva, Belinsky requested contributors who could afford it not to ask Nekrasov for payment for their work, since Nekrasov had exhausted his funds in getting the almanac published. Like its predecessor it was again a manifesto of the new Realism. Its general theme was the plight of the lower classes. As in his second almanac, Nekrasov was both publisher and editor, although again the tone of the collection was set by Belinsky. His article, "Thoughts and Notes on Russian Literature," praised literature as a great educational force. Education, he claimed, makes people equal. The collaborators Belinsky and Nekrasov deserve great credit for their discovery of a new writer for this collection, namely Dostoyevsky, whose *Poor Folks* they took to be an example of the style and ideology of the "natural school." [13] Nekrasov's poems included were: "On the Road," "The Drunkard," "Happy to See," and "Cradle Song."

The poems he contributed mark a distinct advance in poetic technique over his earlier verses. His satire is much more biting in this collection, and there is little comedy for entertainment's sake, but rather a new, sharp tone of criticism. Gogol's influence in theme and approach is still evident; one might even say with Chukovsky that all his poems in this almanac represent differing types of Chichikov.[14] This almanac also marks a milestone in Nekrasov's relations with the government. The censorship was so worried that three censors had to sign the release for publication. The infamous "Third Section," the secret police, took note of it and from this time on kept the editor-publisher under surveillance. The long and hard battle with the censors, whose tricks and traps he came to know, was invaluable experience for the young poet.[15]

Nekrasov's fourth and last publishing venture before taking over a regular periodical was the humorous almanac *The First of April*, 1846. It was a comic illustrated almanac of which Nekrasov was again both editor and publisher, and this time also the chief contributor. He included his own farces, poems, satiric *feuilletons*, and various parodies. In these items he carried on a running polemic with the serf-owners, usually in the form of broad, crude humor. The new bourgeoisie also came under attack for its pretensions and affections, but most of all for its great greed for money. Not all the material consisted of sharply critical attacks, since much of it was mere spoof of various contemporary foibles such as the love for card-playing that swept St. Petersburg at this time.

III The Contemporary

With this less than weighty effort, Nekrasov's period of apprenticeship in publishing comes to an end. In February, 1846, Belinsky left Krayevsky's *Notes of the Fatherland* and remained for a short time without a proper organ in which to express his ideas. In the summer of that year, Nekrasov and I. I. Panayev set out to find a periodical which they could buy. There was no question of founding a new organ, since the government had regulation according to which no new periodicals or magazines could be established.[16] At the end of September, Nekrasov finally reached an agreement with Pletnëv, the editor-publisher of *The Contemporary*, a monthly magazine founded in 1836 by Pushkin. The magazine had gone down hill rapidly after Pushkin's death, since Pletnëv's management of it was conservative and ineffectual. By 1846 it had only 233 subscribers. Nevertheless, the negotiations for its acquisition were long and wearisome.[17] A complicating factor was the attitude of the government. Ever since publication of the almanacs, the censors had been aware of Nekrasov and his activities; Belinsky was in even greater official disfavor. The government refused outright to let Nekrasov or Belinsky be named editor or publisher. As a solution Panayev was named publisher, and A. V. Nikitenko, a member of the St. Petersburg censorship committee, was named editor. Panayev made the largest single investment in purchasing the publishing rights. Nekrasov contributed what he could, but was forced to borrow five thousand rubles from Herzen's wife in order to finance the first issue.

The title "Contemporary," although inherited from Pushkin and Pletnëv, was for Nekrasov and his colleagues a slogan and a program. It suggested to friend and foe alike a new departure: the turn to the immediate problems of the day, the renunciation of Romanticism, of historicizing and idealizing nationalism, and a new emphasis on the social and political conditions of contemporary Russia. Because of the pressure of competition, the new management started immediately to try to persuade certain writers to sign exclusive contracts with *The Contemporary*. This would mean that these writers could no longer contribute to Krayevsky's *Notes of the Fatherland*, for example. The plan was only partly successful, since some key figures, among them Turgenev and most of the Moscow group, continued to publish where they pleased. The battle with competition was fought on many fronts. Krayevsky tried all means, fair and foul, to harm the new periodical. He sent agents to Moscow to dissuade the Moscow writers from contributing to Nekrasov's magazine. He wrote letters, published open attacks in the pages of his own publications, and made the public pronouncement that the withdrawal from his paper of such writers as Belinsky, Nekrasov, and Panayev meant but a slight loss. Even before the first issue of the new *Contemporary* had appeared, he published a sharp polemic against the announced editorial policy and the list of contributors.

Thus the new *Contemporary* was born in battle and nurtured in polemic struggle. But its triumph was assured by the quality of its contributors. The first issues contained contributions by Herzen, including his well-known "Who is to Blame"; "An Ordinary Story" by Goncharov; the first tales of *A Sportsman's Notes* by Turgenev; poems by Nekrasov and Ogarëv; and of course articles by Belinsky, including his important "A Look at Russian Literature for 1846," which was not only again a manifesto of the new Realism, but also contained a clear political tendency, since Belinsky unmistakably, though in Aesopian language, called the problem of serfdom the central and basic issue of Russian culture. Nikitenko, the nominal editor, contributed little. He was wanted only for his name and his connections and was from the beginning supposed only to play the role of a figurehead. At times he forgot this and started to reject or accept contributions to the magazine, thereby testing the tact and diplomacy of the real editor. From the first Nekrasov and Panayev had intended the monthly as a proper forum for Belinsky. But when Belinsky, early in 1847, proposed to Nekrasov that he receive one-third of the income of the periodical, he was much embittered for a short while by Nekrasov's refusal. Panayev agreed with Nekrasov that Belinsky was and should be the leading figure for the new enterprise, but they also agreed that he should neither share in the profits nor be a manager.[18] Belinsky received generous sums for his contributions, but he had neither the skill nor the temperament to handle an administrative position. In April, 1847, Nekrasov raised ten thousand rubles for Belinsky, so that the ailing critic could go abroad. This sum represented more than the magazine was to earn for several years. But it was well worth it, since Belinsky was the inspiration and guiding light of the magazine. He enjoyed a free hand in setting the periodical's tone and in choosing articles to be published.

The success of the new enterprise was immediate. The planners had calculated that they would break even if they succeeded in securing two thousand subscribers. For the year 1847, they had just that number. The next year, the number of subscribers rose to more than three thousand.[19] (For comparison, Krayevsky's *Notes of the Fatherland,* thanks to Belinsky, had four thousand subscribers for the year 1847.) These statistics tell little about the financial condition of the magazine. From the beginning in 1846 to the end in 1866 the magazine was in financial difficulties. The contract for the publishing rights with Pletnëv called for exorbitant annual payments. Belinsky made quite unreasonable demands—and received unreasonable amounts for his work. Nekrasov had to go into debt in order to make the original purchase of the rights, he was often forced to pay higher honorariums than the competition, and he had to pay bribes in order to smooth the path through the office of censorship. Throughout the life of the magazine, Nekrasov was generous to a fault in giving advances and subsidies to struggling young writers. After the death of Dobroliubov, the monthly took over the support of the surviving younger brothers. When Chernyshevsky was sent to Siberia, his wife and children received regular payments. Constant indebtedness made Nekrasov irregular at times in his payments to the regular contributors, with whom he could often drive a hard bargain, as he himself admitted.[20] Accounts and records were in constant disorder, with the result that almost every issue meant a crisis. Frequent loans were necessary, and Nekrasov often helped the publication out from his own private funds. He told Chernyshevsky that he put more into the monthly than he took out of it. Advances to contributors or co-editors were often made privately by Nekrasov without any written record. Some writers took advantage of this and collected months ahead for works which they had promised. In January, 1864, approximately 35,000 rubles were loaned out as advances or prepayments.

IV *The Struggle with Censorship*

If financial worries had been Nekrasov's only problem, his life as editor would have been comfortable and idyllic. Although it is true that even today no one knows where the necessary funds came from and how the periodical survived financially, the mystery surrounding his successful contests with the censorship has been dispelled to a great extent. Nekrasov knew his enemies well, knew how to think like them and ahead of them, and understood their fears and weaknesses. For a time during the 1860's the censors permitted Nekrasov to publish: in part to keep up a liberal façade for their operations, in part because of the theory advanced by Valuyev and adopted by his successor A. E. Timashev that it was better to keep the magazine in the open and not invite underground, illegal activity. It is even possible that Nekrasov understood this game and cooperated by agreeing to hold his policies within certain limits in exchange for official permission to publish an opposition magazine. There were several censors who played a double game, since they acted as Nekrasov's informers, keeping him posted on the proceedings of the censorship board. In return, the editor-poet wined and dined them, took them with him on hunting trips, and printed their literary efforts under pseudonyms. From the diary of V. M. Lazarevsky, a member of both the council for internal affairs and the office for the press, we learn some of the sordid details. He told how Nekrasov bribed a certain M. N. Tutunov; how another censor, Elenev, published with Nekrasov under a pseudonym. His diary reveals a murky mess of unprincipled corruption, venality, greed, and duplicity.[21] Lazarevsky was a hypocrite who despised Nekrasov but wore the mask of friendship. He was a frequent dinner guest of the poet and also accompanied Nekrasov on hunting trips. In effect, they used each other.

The story of Lazarevsky's dubious dealings is merely sordid, but the tale of Nekrasov's relations with F. M. Tolstoy also has its amusing sides. F. M. Tolstoy, who wrote under the name of Rostislav, was a nobleman with court connections, many noble relatives, little money, much leisure, and ambitions beyond his abilities. He harbored an unrequited love for literature. He wrote copiously and badly: songs, operas, cantatas, novels, dramas, *feuilletons*, and reviews. He carried on a wide correspondence, much of which was devoted to attempts to get his works published. In political matters he was reactionary, in favor of serfdom, and a great admirer of Czar Nicholas I. As a publicist he was a close comrade of Bulgarin and his *Northern Bee*, and he often attacked the members of the "natural school." Saltykov-Shchedrin paid him back in kind in a devastating article in *The Contemporary* in 1863. But Tolstoy, who could never agree with himself and was always of two minds about everything, felt strongly attracted to both Nekrasov and Saltykov-Shchedrin and wrote them both long, friendly letters. He flattered Nekrasov and claimed to "love" his poems. Nekrasov treated him coolly—until he needed him, when he exploited him shamelessly. Actually F. M. Tolstoy was a typical government official of the time. Many of them were schizophrenic, for they worshipped what they forbade and admired what they burned. They had little sense of anything but mechanical service to the government and its regulations. They entertained private opinions in clear opposition to the statutes and were quite conscious of defending a cause that was decaying.

The sad state of the bureaucracy in Russia in this period needs a note of explanation. The Decembrist Revolt of December, 1825, is the starting point usually assigned by historians. Members of the aristocracy, which till then had been the support of Church and Crown, turned upon the czar in open, armed revolt. Even though it was but a small fraction of the nobility that participated, the shock effect on Czar Nicholas was tremendous. Thereafter he put his faith in the bureaucracy, which, to be sure, was largely recruited at the upper levels from the aristocracy, but which served at his pleasure, since the czar could make or break any civil servant at will. The bureaucrats were now set to the task of running the country and of guarding the throne and the imperial interests. The great expansion of the number of government officials, especially in sections such as censorship, may be attributed in large part to the czar's reaction to the Decembrist revolt.

The censors' "double thinking" and their thoroughgoing inconsistency made them susceptible to Nekrasov's wiles. He was even able to use them—the agents of repressive government—at times as defenders of the democratic press, in which some of them longed inordinately to be published. It was relatively easy for Nekrasov to exploit Tolstoy's great urge to publish and become famous, as well as to take advantage of his vacillating judgment. Tolstoy interceded for Nekrasov when he purchased the rights to the monthly *Notes of the Fatherland.* In return for favors rendered, Tolstoy demanded that he be allowed to become a contributor. He did in fact receive as a bribe the position of music and theater critic. By threatening certain issues of the monthly—Tolstoy was after all still a censor—he obtained bribes and concessions from Nekrasov, who published his opera reviews, but only after rewriting them, shortening them, and doing all in his power to bring them up to the level of the magazine. Finally an end was put to this low comedy by the loss of Tolstoy's government position in October, 1871. Nekrasov soon thereafter freed himself of the necessity of publishing Tolstoy's nonsense. But Tolstoy took his dismissal badly, and he would never admit that his articles were really bribes.[22]

In addition to the original works of literature which *The Contemporary* brought out every month, there were other sections of the monthly that also became popular. A very high standard was set by the section of literary criticism and bibliography. This was at first under the direction of Belinsky, who published in it his articles and reviews. Occasionally Nekrasov also contributed to this section, but its original tone was set by Belinsky. The science of the day also occupied a significant section of the periodical. Translations of the works of foreign scientists appeared in these pages, together with articles on geography, astronomy, zoology, and chemistry. As a kind of appendage there was a section called "Miscellany," a title chosen to lead the censors astray, since, under the guise of entertaining *feuilletons,* attacks on serfdom and other evils could be hidden in it. In this section appeared a long article describing the pitiful conditions of the peasants in Ireland. But the similarities with the state of things in Russia were so obvious that any alert reader could easily see the point.

In its philosophical stand the monthly was aggressively atheistic and materialistic. Many articles were devoted to a criticism of contemporary religious life, and just as many to a refutation of idealism, especially that based on German philosophy. One must not forget that *The Contemporary* during its early years under Nekrasov was a lone liberal voice crying in a conservative wilderness. Most of the periodicals and journals of the day were singing the praises of the regime, or they were indulging in Slavophil mystiques of the Russian soul and viewing with complacent pride the advantages of serfdom with its blessings, its patience and piety, and the splendid patriarchal system which protected the poor *muzhik.* If the voices of the radical revolutionaries seem shrill at times, one must remember that they were greatly outnumbered by the glorifiers of the grand old Russian way of life.[23]

In view of his isolated position it is not surprising that Nekrasov frequently exhorted the members of the "natural school" to stand firm and be of one mind. As has already been mentioned, Nekrasov very early tried to bind certain writers to his magazine with exclusive contracts. In 1856 he made a second and last attempt to obtain agreements for exclusive contribution to his monthly, this time with Turgenev, L. N. Tolstoy, Ostrovsky, and Grigorovich. Beginning in January, 1857, the four authors were to print their works exclusively in *The Contemporary* for a period of four years. In addition to the usual payments for publication of writings submitted, they were to divide equally among them two-thirds of the income of the monthly after expenses. It was, of course, more than just a financial arrangement, since it represented a last attempt to paper over the differences between the liberals and the radicals. The contract was invalid after a very short time; given the nature of the people involved, it could not have been otherwise. In 1858 Tolstoy ceased to publish with Nekrasov. Early in 1858 Nekrasov and Panayev, seeing that the contract was not being honored by the authors theoretically bound by it, declared the agreement to have lapsed. It was the last attempt of its kind made by the editors of *The Contemporary,* and its failure was symptomatic of the coming open break between the liberals and the radicals.

V *The Death of Belinsky*

Belinsky's death in 1847 deprived Nekrasov of an irreplaceable mentor and critic. Belinsky had been the inspiration of the enterprise. I. I. Panayev continued to contribute and help as much as he could, but he was both lazy and dissipated. Although frivolous and rather superficial, he had absorbed enough of Belinsky's spirit to be of some comfort to Nekrasov, whom he supported even when he did not understand him. Sometime during the mid 1840's his pretty wife, Avdotia, whom Panayev neglected, became the mistress and common-law wife of Nekrasov. For the next fifteen or sixteen years a strange *ménage à trois* existed in the spacious quarters of the Panayevs. The poet loved Avdotia with an intense and tormented passion. She inspired many of his tenderest lyrics, but she also caused him much pain. She was a charming, intelligent, and affable woman and a splendid hostess who entertained all the great writers of the mid-century—Turgenev, Goncharov, Leo Tolstoy, Dostoyevsky, Ostrovsky—as well as many less well-known ones. There is an oft-quoted saying that if the roof of her living room had collapsed during one of her receptions, Russian literature would have been destroyed. She collaborated with Nekrasov on both his long novels, assisted him in most of his undertakings, took his side in the frequent discussions which arose in the mixed group that gathered under her roof, and nursed Dobroliubov during his last illness. Her memoirs, written many years later, are a fine source of intimate glimpses of the poet and his circle. But they must be read with some caution, since her judgments are often partisan and her memory not always trustworthy. She was uniformly unfair to Turgenev, whom she could not stand, and her opinions of other people were frequently arbitrary and are therefore unreliable. Readers who are interested may test her literary ability by reading *Dead Lake* and *Three Countries of the World,* parts of which are wholly from her hand.[24]

Avdotia Panayeva was, of course, no replacement for Belinsky. In the dark years that followed, between 1848 and 1855, Nekrasov had to rely primarily on himself, both as editor and critic, in managing *The Contemporary.* Of necessity he collaborated with the liberals: Botkin, Annenkov, Druzhinin, and Turgenev. They were aware of the evils in Russian society and advocated reform, but gentle, gradual reform that would not cause any violent upheaval. Their cooperation with Nekrasov was the result as much of the heritage of Belinsky as it was of their respect for Nekrasov, whom they admired as businessman and editor, but held in low esteem as poet. They did tolerate him during this period, and they supported many of his decisions. Since *The Contemporary* continued to be the leading periodical of the time, it was obviously to their advantage to be associated with it. For the poet, it was a time of constant struggle. Only his unusual qualities saved him from disaster. He was capable of an incredible amount of work, was full of wiles and stratagems, knew when to be aggressive and inflexible and when to give in or compromise. Since his magazine had become the symbol and rallying point for the radical intelligentsia, he was a favorite target of the censors. In 1849 both he and Panayev were threatened with arrest and the foreclosure of the monthly. More than once they had to report in person to the police to defend themselves and their publication. In addition to this type of harassment, the censors blocked publication of material after it had been printed and was ready for distribution. It has been estimated that during the "dark seven years" (1848–55) more than a million words were refused publication in *The Contemporary.* The obvious consequence of such harassment was that Nekrasov was constantly pressed for material, that is, for harmless material that could be published. His novels in collaboration with

Avdotia Panayeva, written in order to fill gaps caused by censorship, were only a partial solution to this problem. Even so, in the case of *Dead Lake,* Nekrasov had to sign a pledge that the novel would end happily with vice punished and virtue rewarded. In his letters during these years one may read the almost pathetic requests for manuscripts that he addressed to his friends. In view of the difficulties he had to overcome, it is astounding how well he succeeded in making his magazine the focus of the best writing of the time. His critical acumen enabled him to sift the hundreds of manuscripts submitted for the best and most enduring contributions. Just as he had once sensed the potential greatness of Dostoyevsky, so did he discover the talent of a then-unknown young writer named L. N. Tolstoy, who sent his first work, *Childhood,* to Nekrasov in July, 1853. Neither Dostoyevsky nor Tolstoy were in any sense kindred spirits of Nekrasov; their specific genius was basically very different from his own. Nevertheless, he was able to appreciate them and boldly introduced them to the reading public.

The testimony of his contemporaries and collaborators confirms the picture of Nekrasov as an astute and competent editor. Antonovich, who for years was co-editor with the poet, went so far as to call him an ideal editor. He stressed the fact that Nekrasov was not personally ambitious, but very modest and undemanding. Mikhailovsky also noted his tolerance and his readiness to help young writers. The editorial board of *The Contemporary,* and later that of *Notes of the Fatherland,* ran smoothly on a cooperative basis. Avdotia Panayeva, who rather enjoyed gossip, reports that there were many disagreements and quarrels among the circle around Belinsky, and later in the group gathered about *The Contemporary.* She relates (or invents) in her memoirs several scenes in which arguments took place, usually with either Turgenev or Botkin playing the role of the villain. But more reliable sources fail to confirm these memories of a woman who herself courted arguments. As responsible editor, Nekrasov had the last word in selecting and arranging the material, and he was constantly making critical judgments and decisions. But he listened to advice and was ready to cooperate and compromise. He made no personal profit from his periodicals, which were constantly in arrears in payments. The deficit of the magazine in

1864 was 19,643 rubles, and the next year 23,307 rubles. The legend of his greed and his unscrupulous dealings with co-workers and contributors stems from slander long since refuted. In general he ran his enterprise like a family of which any serious contibutor of talent could become a member.[25]

Near the end of the dark seven years, in 1854, a new personality joined the circle of *The Contemporary,* namely Chernyshevsky, a critic who was to exert considerable influence on Russian letters during the next decade. In many ways he reminds one of Belinsky, whose heritage he believed he was continuing. He had had university training, was very well-read—especially in Belinsky and Herzen—and from his student days on was a convinced and avowed revolutionary. He was aggressively socialistic and revolutionary in all his publications, so that his appeal was confined to like-minded spirits, but he never held the same commanding position that once had been Belinsky's. His militant materialism and positivism were expressed early and vigorously, so that from the beginning there was no doubt at all about where he stood. From the first evening at the Panayevs' on he was anathema to the liberals, whom he offended both by his attitude and his outspoken views. After all, the liberals were all aristocrats who had lived and studied abroad, and they were instinctively suspicious of the *raznochinsty.* In all of his literary criticism the predominance of social and political considerations was so striking that to the liberals he seemed deficient in esthetics if not downright antiesthetic. In less than a year he became an intimate friend of Nekrasov, who came to rely on him more and more, at first in matters of literary criticism and then in editorial questions. He progressed from contributor to co-editor so rapidly that older friends of the poet were offended by his sudden acceptance too. When Nekrasov went to Europe for several months in 1856, he left *The Contemporary* in the hands of Chernyshevsky, much to the annoyance of the older group, who had been loyal in their way for so long. Botkin and Druzhinin attempted to block the move and tried to persuade Nekrasov to put Grigor'ev in charge. Turgenev joined them in not trying to conceal his displeasure. But Nekrasov remained firm, entrusted everything to Chernyshevsky, and left for Europe convinced that he had made the right choice.

VI *The Break with the Liberals*

The positivistic and revolutionary trend of the monthly had long been a source of irritation to the liberals, and with Chernyshevsky as managing editor they found new cause for complaint. On the eve of the Peasant Reform, new hope welled up in the hearts of the liberals, who expected great things from the impending changes and reforms. Everyone breathed easier in the comparative calm and relative lack of repression following the Crimean War. The need for calls to violent revolution to change conditions seemed to the liberals to be past. But to Nekrasov and Chernyshevsky the necessity for really profound reform in the organization of Russian life remained in all its urgency. They expected little from a reform dictated from above, planned by reactionary landowners, and carried out by the legal and military authority of an autocratic regime. Even radicals like Herzen pinned their hopes to a reform instituted by government authority and attacked the *Contemporary* circle for still insisting that the revolution must come from below.

The Contemporary added to its inner circle in 1858 another important critic, N. A. Dobroliubov, who like Chernyshevsky started as a contributor of articles and critiques and soon advanced to a central position in the monthly. Dobroliubov was even more vehement than Chernyshevsky in his assertion of the primacy of social and political criteria in judging all literature and art. He soon became the leading exponent of the functional approach to literature that had entered Russian literary criticism with Belinsky. Accepting the basic tenets of Chernyshevsky's thesis in *The Esthetic Relation of Art to Reality*, he believed that literature should faithfully reproduce contemporary social phenomena. Moreover, the artist, in the Dobroliubovian esthetic, was obliged to deal with pressing social problems; his art was supposed to contribute to the welfare of his society by solving, or at least posing, the problems upon which social progress depended. Dobroliubov looked for socially relevant statements in his analysis of literature. The importance of literature, he tells us, "lies in propaganda, and the merit of it is determined by what it propagates, and how it propagates it." [26] Since he evaluated literature exclusively on the basis of how effectively it embodied the social convictions of the radical intelligentsia, much of Dobroliubov's criticism is not properly literary criticism at all. Works of literature were merely the occasion for discussing the problems of Russia: the tyranny of the czarist government, the emancipation of the serfs, the weakness of libralism, and the misery of the oppressed. Dobroliubov rejected reforms imposed from above and looked to the *narod* as the hope of revolution and the repository of Russia's real strength. The increasing unrest among the peasants and the violence of the peasant revolts seemed to confirm his hopes. The ultimate goal of his journalistic efforts was to foster a revolutionary situation, and he used the literary works of his day in order to propagandize the need for a cleansing transformation of society. Literature mattered only in so far as it contributed to this goal.

The regular pages of *The Contemporary* were not well adapted to his purposes and were too closely under the scrutiny of the censors. With Nekrasov's cooperation he soon became the principal editor of a satiric appendage to the monthly, called "The Whistle." In this section he was able to express himself more adequately, although usually in Aesopian language. The favored position of the young seminarist was a further annoyance to the liberals, with whom he openly and stubbornly disagreed. Neither Turgenev, nor Tolstoy, who came to the capital and became acquainted with the *Contemporary* group upon his return from the Crimean War, could stand Dobroliubov.[27] Nekrasov, and in her own way also Mme. Panayeva, sought to mediate between the factions and to placate the older group while defending the intellectual positions of the young radicals. For a few years, from Nekrasov's return from Europe until 1860, an uneasy truce prevailed.

The open and public rupture of relations did not develop until the year before the expected Peasant Reform, 1860. Turgenev and his friends broke with Nekrasov and his circle with bitterness and finality. Several public reasons were given, one of them being the assertion that Nekrasov had been irregular in his payments to Turgenev, another that Nekrasov had refused to prevent the publishing of an article by Dobroliubov that was unfavorable to Turgenev. But the real causes were deeper and were, as has been suggested above, mostly of an ideological nature. In the long run it was impossible to reconcile such opposing views, and it is a tribute to Nekrasov's skill as mediator and conciliator that he was able to keep such disparate spirits together for so long. He lost his most famous and popular writers, but he preferred this loss to abandoning his principles and those friends who supported these principles. Ostrovsky, Saltykov-Shchedrin, N. Uspensky, G. Uspensky, and Pomialovsky are some of the writers who now became regular contributors.

The year of the emancipation of the serfs, 1861, which was greeted by eulogies from the liberals and passed over in silent scorn by the radical revolutionaries (it was not even mentioned in *The Contemporary*), was an exceedingly difficult time for Nekrasov. Dobroliubov, whom the poet had come to love like a son, died after a long illness; and Chernyshevsky, on whom the poet counted both for friendship and intellectual support, was imprisoned and later exiled to Siberia. In this same year I. I. Panayev died. The final break with Avdotia Panayeva, delayed perhaps by Dobroliubov's illness, followed shortly thereafter. *The Contemporary*, after several preliminary warnings, was suspended for eight months. The abolition of serfdom had led, just as the radicals had predicted, to a whole series of peasant revolts.[28] The nervous government, which broke up these revolts by the ruthless use of troops, was not in a mood for carping criticism or sniping from the radical Left. When the period of suspension was over and the monthly was allowed to appear again, Nekrasov remained unrepentant and did not soften his tone, but on the contrary in defiance published Chernyshevsky's novel *What is to be Done?* With the support of new co-workers such as Eliseyev, Antonovich, Pypin, and Saltykov-Shchedrin he was able during the next few years to keep ahead of the censors and his creditors by dint of hard work, but we can only guess at the cost in nervous energy and wasted time. The magazine had gradually become a way of life for Nekrasov. We can assess the full measure of his dedication to the enterprise by his actions following Karakozov's attempt to assassinate the czar in April, 1866. To the dismay of his friends and the delight of his enemies he wrote a most humbly subservient and loyally submissive poem to the "Hangman of Poland," the hated Murav'ëv, and read in the aristocratic English Club a poem in praise of the man who had saved the czar's life.[29] This apparent renunciation of his former views deceived no one. *The Contemporary* was permanently banned.

VII Notes of the Fatherland

Nekrasov could not long live and be himself without a periodical to publish. In the same year, 1866, he began negotiations for the purchase of the editoral rights to the moderate, soothingly liberal *Notes of the Fatherland,* still in the hands of his old competitor and opponent Krayevsky. The negotiations were protracted and in the end only partly successful, since Krayevsky's name was retained as publisher of the periodical. Nekrasov had to agree to give half the income of the monthly to Krayevsky. Nekrasov was able to obtain a free hand with regard to editorial policy but only on the condition that, after two preliminary warnings from the censors, Krayevsky could intervene in the management of the monthly. The further condition was appended to the contract, that Nekrasov was not to criticize the newspaper *The Voice,* another publication owned by Krayevsky. Nekrasov never ceased trying to remove Krayevsky's name from the periodical. The government rejected several requests of the poet to replace Krayevsky's name with that of Saltykov-Shchedrin. Nevertheless Nekraskov had once more an organ which he could direct. He lost no time in changing the character of the magazine, which soon appeared as a natural and consistent continuation of *The Contemporary.* Once more there was a forum for the radical revolutionaries and for the *narodniki.* Once again Nekrasov appeared as the leader and representative of the revolutionary intelligentsia, who rallied around *Notes of the Fatherland* as they once had *The Contemporary.* It should be noted, however, that the radical intelligentsia of the 1860's and 1870's was not monolithic in its opinions. On the contrary, it was divided into several different camps. Nekrasov cooperated with the *narodniki,* for example, without entirely sharing their political opinions. The belief was held by many of the *narodniki* that heroes, or leaders of the intelligentsia, would bring about the revolutionary goals which they held. They believed in reforms led from above by volunteer intellectuals who could "go to the people" (hence their name), educate and enlighten them, and lead them to victory. Nekrasov agreed with Chernyshevsky and Dobroliubov that the common people were and should be the bearers of their own salvation, and that as they became better educated and more politically aware they would achieve their goals by themselves. Nevertheless, for several years the *narodniki* published in *Notes of the Fatherland.*

The new management of the monthly soon made a success of what had been a failing periodical with barely two thousand subscribers. New allies and collaborators appeared on the scene, the most notable of whom was Saltykov-Shchedrin, the great satirist. Not all the staff of the old *Contemporary* was carried over into the new enterprise. M. Antonovich, Dobroliubov's successor as co-editor, and Iu. Zhukovsky were not retained, partly because of pressure from the office of censorship, partly because they demanded broader powers in directing the monthly. They expressed their bitterness at what they considered unfair treatment in a series of rude and baseless attacks. Pypin, perhaps out of a sense of solidarity with them, also withdrew. Older contributors such as A. N. Ostrovsky, G. I. Uspensky, F. M. Reshetnikov, D. I. Pisarev, and N. K. Mikhailov continued to publish with Nekrasov. Soon other well-known authors were attracted to the magazine, among them V. A. Sleptsov, V. M. Garshin, D. N. Mamin-Sibiriak, A. N. Pleshcheyev, and S. Ia. Nadson. Foreign literature was represented by many translations from the works of Victor Hugo and Emile Zola, among others.

Each issue was divided into two parts: Literature and articles on contemporary science, and a news and commentary section which dealt with social and political problems. In the latter section the peasant question was the chief topic. The consequences of the Peasant Reform were still the burning issue for the radical journals. The land had not been given to the peasants, but sold to them. The lawsuits over the division of the land, the question of taxes, dues, payments, and discrimination in favor of the former serf-owners—all this led to the impoverishment of the peasants, their restlessness and confusion. Nekrasov's new organ continued its struggle against these chaotic conditions by attacking not only the obvious exploiters, such as the great landowners, but the whole system of government that fostered the misery of the *narod.* Quite naturally the government censorship closely and suspiciously followed each issue of *Notes of the Fatherland.* In spite of alliances and underhand arrangements such as that with F. Tolstoy, in 1874 a whole issue of 8,220 copies was prohibited while in proof and then totally destroyed.

Not all that appeared in the pages of *Notes of the Fatherland* was radical, revolutionary, and suspect in the eyes of the censors. Liberal, even conservative authors published their articles and stories in the magazine. In the 1870's Dostoyevsky and L. Tolstoy published once again under the editorship of Nekrasov, without, however, reaching any reconcilation with him. Tolstoy's motives in publishing with Nekrasov again were not the result of any renewal of their old friendship, but stemmed rather from the desire to reach a large and influential audience.[30] Nekrasov was delighted to have such a great and famous author appear in his pages again. During the 1870's the poet welcomed to an unprecedented extent writers whose political views he did not share, although we do not need to conclude from this that his basic attitudes had changed in any way. His main motive seems to have been the desire to achieve quality, regardless of its source, while placing less exclusive emphasis on political considerations.

It is not that *Notes of the Fatherland* had renounced polemics altogether. On the contrary, the late 1860's and early 1870's saw the monthly engaged in editorial warfare on a broad front; much of this was carried on by the co-editors Saltykov-Shchedrin and Eliseyev, but obviously with the approval of Nekrasov. Even other radical journals felt obliged to enter the lists with wearisome polemics. For the modern reader most of the issues involved are not meaningful. However, at the time what now seems trivial was not a quibble, but a topic of importance capable of generating heated disputes. The press was not only engaged in the discussion of the burning problems of the day but was also equally concerned with the personalities and personal lives of those involved in controversy. The identification of the person with his political position goes back to Belinsky and the formation of the intelligentsia in the 1840's.[31] Conservatives, liberals, and radicals all agreed that the personality of the writer was involved in the views he stated. Therefore the resulting polemics dealt as much with the motives and character of the persons writing as it did with the opinions expressed. The personal attacks on Nekrasov never ceased. Even authors such as G. Uspensky, whom he had sponsored and helped financially, turned against him and published unfounded invective. Uspensky's calumny has long since been disproved—in point of fact he owed the poet more than two thousand rubles—but the affair is symptomatic for the conditions of literary warfare at the time.

The constant attacks wearied and embittered Nekrasov, but they did not deter him from pursuit of his main task. Most of the time he did not personally answer the diatribes directed against him, leaving this task to his co-workers. His stand was clear to all and his principles were known so that he did not feel called upon to formulate them in expository essays or defend them at every opportunity; his work spoke for itself. For thirty years he was the editor of a great periodical. This alone ensures him a place of honor in the history of Russian letters.

CHAPTER 3

Verses: *The Harvest of a Dozen Years*

> As if his own on his body he bears
> The wounds and woe of his native land. (II, 12)

ONLY that writer has any claim to the respect and sympathy of the reader who stirs his heart and awakens his dissatisfaction with all that is base and mean, who treats serious social questions, and in whom all his energy, thought and sense of truth are harmonious" (X, 247).

The first collection of Nekrasov's poems was published in 1856 under the unassuming title of *Verses*. It was a year of several publications of collected poems. Books by Fet, Nikitin, and Ogarëv appeared at nearly the same time. For the first time since 1848 it was possible to risk such an undertaking, since there was a brief slackening of censorship after the death of Nicholas I in the spring of 1855. The years of prose, prophesied by Belinsky, were brought to a close in a brilliant mid-century revival of verse. To be sure, Nekrasov had published most of the poems contained in the collection before, but now for the first time all the poems which he wished to present to the public were gathered into one volume. The death of the czar seemed to inspire Nekrasov. The first hint of any plan for a volume of his collected verse appears in a reference in a letter by Turgenev to Nekrasov of April, 1855. Nekrasov's resurgence as a poet, in spite of ill health, the death of a second child, and bitter quarrels with Avdotia Panayeva, dates from the spring of this year. When the book appeared in October, 1856, it contained twenty-one poems from the years 1845 to 1849, twenty-one from 1850 to 1853, twenty-two dating from 1854 to 1855, and nine from 1856.

The success of the volume was immediate and sensational. Nothing like it had been seen in literary circles since the death of

Pushkin. During October, five hundred copies were sold in St. Petersburg within two days. At the end of two weeks, fourteen hundred copies had been sold. By the end of November, the original price of one and one-half rubles had risen to six rubles because of the great demand. The whole edition was sold out in a few weeks. However the office of censorship forbade a new printing as well as any reprinting of the poems in periodicals. In addition, it was forbidden to mention either the book or the author in the press, so that there were no public notices and, of course, no critical reviews. The news of the astonishing success reached and amazed Nekrasov while he was abroad. He quite sincerely believed that he was an obscure poet whose fame, if any, rested on his journalistic achievements. His letters from the fall of 1856 express his genuine surprise and delight. As late as 1855 he had written a poem beginning: "Unknown am I," in which he both admitted his obscurity and proclaimed proudly that he did not write for the public.

The poet was forced to resort to many dodges and stratagems in order to get the book published at all. Even while the manuscript was in the hands of the printer, the poet was compelled to make many changes and accept alterations and deletions. The final version as permitted by the censors differs considerably from that which Nekrasov submitted to his printer.[1] When the volume of some 225 pages did appear, the censors were horrified all over again and were dismayed by the impact of the book as well as by its contents. A special report was submitted to the Minister of the Interior because Chernyshevsky, in charge of *The Contemporary* during Nekrasov's travels in Western Europe, reprinted some of the poems (notably "Poet and Citizen" and "The Forgotten Village") in its pages. Because of the strict prohibition of the reprinting of any poems from the book, the management of the magazine was sternly warned and even threatened with suppression. The effect of all these repressive measures was to increase the popularity of *Verses.* Manuscripts of the poems were circulated widely, and foreign presses printed copies in a small format which would fit the pockets of Russian tourists returning from western Europe.

The arrangement of the poems was a matter of great concern to the poet, who devoted much thought and care to the final form of the book. From the time of the contract with a Moscow publisher toward the end of 1855 until the book appeared a year later, Nekrasov, in spite of his illness and his trip abroad, managed to write new poems, rewrite old, correct, fill gaps due to deletions of censorship, and decide on an arrangement of the poems. In the end he chose a sequence that disregarded chronology and ordered the poems for their composite effect. The final arrangement consisted of an introductory poem, "Poet and Citizen," printed in heavier, larger print than the rest of the book in order to emphasize its programmatic character, followed by four sections: the first with eleven poems, opening with "On the Road" and closing with "The Schoolboy," brought mostly "poems of the people," some lyric-descriptive, some narrative in style; the second section of fourteen poems contained only satirical verses. The third section had but one poem, "Sasha," with its picture of the contemporary intelligentsia. The fourth section contained mostly lyric poems, with intimate, confessional poems alternating with civic poems in such a way that the poet's intent became obvious: there is no real distinction between the two types of poem, since they are interrelated and one shades off imperceptibly into the other. It is in fact impossible to distinguish them at times, since the poems which state most clearly his attitude toward poetry and his understanding of the poet's role are also the ones which declare most frankly his sense of social engagement. Childhood, friendship, love, nature: these are the traditional lyric themes that appear here, but with Nekrasov they are always interwoven with social criticism in such a way that to distinguish between civic and personal poems is often not appropriate.

For Nekrasov and his circle the relation of the poet's ego to his environment was immediate, basic, and involved. For many other poets of the period, such as Fet, Tiutchev, or A. K. Tolstoy, the relationship was more abstract, contemplative, and remote from topical problems. Their concern was more with timeless verities than with the social conditions about them. It is perhaps an oversimplification to reduce the difference between Nekrasov and the advocates of "pure poetry" to the formula of social versus metaphysical concern, but it does express the fundamental distinguishing attitudes. For Nekrasov, Dobroliubov, and Chernyshevsky the problematic relations of a poet to society and to the proper function of the poet in that society were not eternal or cosmic but were historically conditioned and closely connected with the sociological facts of any given period. Thus the final section of *Verses* documents both the poet's personality and his principles while emphasizing their interrelation, if not their identity. In most of the poems of the fourth section there is a broadening of the personal and confessional into the general and representative within the scope of a given poem. Often the expression of the lyric hero's emotions or views serves only as a point of departure for a picture of contemporary conditions. Thus not all the poems loosely designated lyric are truly confessional poems, since they do not necessarily give Nekrasov's own views, but often only those of the fictional speaker of the verses. If it is the author himself speaking, then he tends to state openly, even tendentiously, his credo, especially in emphatic form at the end of the poem. If it is the voice of a fictional lyric hero, then the tendency of the poem is to generalize and typify, whatever narrative element or other specific starting point there may have been. The effect of the grouping of the poems chosen by Nekrasov is to keep as a dominant note the summons to active participation in life and its problems, thus echoing and reinforcing the theme of the introductory poem of the book.[2] The final poem of the book, "Be Silent, Muse of Vengeance and Sorrow," is a kind of last will and testament—Nekrasov believed sincerely that he would soon die and never publish again. The tone of the volume, set by the didactic introductory poem, is very serious. But the poet did include, especially in the second section, some humorous satiric verses and took care to end the first section with the optimistic "The Schoolboy." Nevertheless, a rather stern and somber note prevails, since even the satiric poems serve the serious purpose of illuminating problems of contemporary life.

Throughout the book, but especially in the poems of daily life and common experience, we note the growing mastery of the poet. In one direction, his power of making the specific become representative and point beyond itself to the general seems to grow with every year. In another direction, his ability to capture in verse the specific nature of concrete objects and to waken them to life in his verse becomes more versatile and refined. The portraits of people, from "The Gardener" of 1845 to "Vlas" of 1854, show an increasing sureness in choosing the significant traits that evoke a complete picture. From the beginning—and here it is difficult to trace a development—Nekrasov was able to locate his figures in a specific environment with great economy of effort. All his fictional persons, or the voice of the author if it is he who is speaking, emerge from a recognizable background, have a visualizable location in time and space, and speak to us from a condition of life that is immediately familiar. Progress or improvement we shall find only when we turn to the longer narrative poems of his later years. But already in a poem such as "Sasha" (1855) we note the ability to evoke a spiritual ambience that harmonizes with the physical surroundings and gives the reader the impression of experiencing a totality. The emphasis on the lyric figure's relation to his environment is a significant feature of Nekrasov's *Verses* that contrasts sharply with most contemporary poetry. When combined, as it usually was, with the immediacy and intimacy resulting from either a dialogue situation or the voice of the lyric "I" in direct address, the unmistakable tonality of a Nekrasov poem is achieved. As an innovator in Russian verse this is one of his greatest contributions.

The first, emphatically positioned and printed poem, "Poet and Citizen" (1856), is remotely reminiscent of Pushkin's famous "Conversation of the Bookseller with the Poet" (1824). But the first impression of formal similarity is soon dispelled by both the tone and the message. The person of the citizen is probably a composite figure derived from Belinsky and Chernyshevsky. The poet bears certain autobiographical features in his relation to his muse and in the fact that he is portrayed as having erred in his youth and as not having achieved his high desire. This element of self-criticism means that the poem may also be located among Nekrasov's "penitent poems," his poems of self-reproach. But the figure of the poet is also a composite one, since it is evidently based in large part on Nekrasov's view of an apostle of "pure poetry." The message of the poem is a clear call to Realism, to the involvement with the dark side of Russian life, and to criticism where it is due. The poet is called to the service of his fatherland as proof of his professed love for it. The poem is at once both a summons to active involvement in life and a statement of Nekrasov's principles of esthetics. Both Dobroliubov and Chernyshevsky prized highly the lines:

> A son cannot quietly gaze
> At the grief of his mother country . . .
> Go into fire for the honor of your native land,
> For your convictions and for love . . .
> Go and perish without reproach.
> You will not die in vain: the cause is good
> If blood does flow beneath it . . .

Much admired and often quoted by Soviet critics are the lines:

> You do not have to be a poet,
> A citizen though you're obliged to be.

This lapidary statement is in the original Russian couched in a rough, prosy style. The emphatic, half-versified statement is, unfortunately, characteristic of this most frankly didactic poem, which fails as art because of the preponderance of sternly stated thesis over artistic transformation. We can identify many features in both form and content which mark the poem as coming from Nekrasov's pen. But the conversation never quite comes alive, since the reader is constantly confronted with the straightforward, unadorned statement of the thesis. The contrast between the positions taken by the avowedly lazy poet and the fervently revolutionary citizen is too crassly emphasized. The result is an impassioned tract. It is still possible to respect the message of the verses, but without admiring them as art.

I *The Question of Genre*

The difficult problem of genre has never been satisfactorily solved with respect to much of Nekrasov's poetry. Most traditional terms are inadequate to classify many of his poems, and critics usually resort to hyphenated compounds when attempting to order his poems according to type. His poems on poetry and the poet's role in life are sometimes mainly didactic, as we have noted in the case of "Poet and Citizen," but since few poems have but a single theme, these same verses shade off into his penitent poems, and these in turn are only partly autobiographical and usually contain other distinctive elements. One of Nekrasov's very short but famous poems is the one beginning "Yesterday at Six O'clock," which will illustrate nicely the mixture of themes in a single work.

> Yesterday at six o'clock
> I went to Senna square;
> There they flogged by knout
> A young peasant woman.
>
> Not a sound came from her breast,
> Only the whip whistled, playing . . .
> And to my muse I said: Behold!
> There is your own, your beloved sister. (1848)

This is a fine example of the poet's use of a deliberate prosaism for a startling effect at the beginning of a poem. These eight lines are usually classified in the category of poems on the sad fate of women in Russia, but the unexpected identification of the poet's muse with the peasant woman illustrates well the tendency toward mixed themes. The prosy preciseness of the beginning combined with the terse, cool language makes this one of his most impressive poems on the condition of women, and at the same time it expresses his sympathy with their suffering.[3]

The poem "Muse" (1851) is in many respects similar to the paradigmatic "Poet and Citizen," although this time the poet did not choose the form of dialogue but preferred to speak in his own person. Nekrasov was well aware that not all poets were chiefly concerned with the pressing problems of the reality about them and knew too that his predecessors had not chosen primarily topical themes. Many of his poems are polemic expressions of his sense of being different from those who sing in clarion notes the praises of some fairylike or semidivine muse. Nekrasov's "Muse" is directly opposed to that of the young Pushkin, whose poem "Muse" ("V Mladenchestve moëm . . . ," 1821) he deliberately echoes in his first few lines. The polemical tone is not directed at Pushkin, however, but rather at the contemporary belated Romanticists who found support for their position in carefully selected verses of Pushkin. Nekrasov's poem is once again a manifesto of Realism and a call to involvement and commitment, but the diction is that of solemn high style[4] and the verse form is that of classical Alexandrines rhymed in couplets. The choice of this form serves the purpose of heightening the contrast between classic form and militant message.

The start of the poem, varying the theme set by Puskin, is as follows:

> No, a beautiful muse singing sweetly
> A mellifluous melody o'er my cradle I do not recall!
> In heavenly beauty, silent as a spirit,
> Flying down from on high, she did not teach
> My youthful voice enchanting harmony
> Nor leave in my cradle a magic flute.

Nekrasov's muse was one of sorrow and suffering, the sad companion of those born to hard labor and chains, a muse of tears and pain. He insisted on this sort of muse with snarling clusters of palatal and sibilant consonants such as the following:

> *. . . toi Muzy plashchushchei, skorbiashchei i*
> *boliashchei*
> *Vsechasno zhazhdushchei, unizenno prosiashchei . . .*

His muse cries for vengeance and calls down God's wrath upon the heads of his enemies. She appears more like an avenging angel than as a conventional, gentle muse. Although Turgenev criticized the repetition of the word "dreams," he claimed to like the poem, attracted perhaps by the high style and pathos. Upon reading it in *The Contemporary* in 1854, the poet A. N. Makov wrote a poem to Nekrasov, advising him to give up angry and accusatory verse. This was one of the first overt moves of the "pure poetry" group against Nekrasov.

Related in theme and attitude is the poem "On the Day of Gogol's Death," originally published without a title, since censorship forbade any mention of Gogol. With a theme taken from Gogol's *Dead Souls* the poem opens:

For happy is the gentle poet—
With little bile and lots of feeling:
For him the friends of tranquil art
Forever have such kind regards.

Nekrasov's attitude toward the meek and mild poet is patently ironical. He prefers the aggressive, engaged poet capable of hate for what is evil as well as love for what is beautiful. The oft-quoted last lines of the poem are: "And how he loved—hating!" To a degree Nekrasov drew here a self-portrait, for he ascribes many of his own characteristics to Gogol, who was actually rather timid. Nekrasov is here drawing a picture of Gogol as he and Belinsky wished he had been. Yet it is true that there is a strong similarity to Gogol's opposition of the gentle poet to the genuine poet who sees the bitter truth in the social realities of contemporary life.[5] The real poet is encouraged by the sounds of irritation and anger which greet his protests and unmaskings of evil. This anger is suggested by the harsh clacking of velars in a line like "A v dikikh krikakh ozoblen'ia." The genuine poet rejoices that he is surrounded by "serious enemies" and is stimulated by their opposition. Such delight in combat is an important ingredient in Nekrasov's own character. With much more justice than in the case of Gogol, who always really wanted to conform, Nekrasov ascribed the same joy in literary warfare to Belinsky in the poem "V. G. Belinsky" 1855):

Nor did he spare the flatterers,
Nor scoundrels, nor idiots either,
Nor "loyal" thieves when wearing
The mask of ardent patriotism! . . .

The savage cry of slander
Did not dismay him . . .

II *Satiric Poems*

The satiric poems of *Verses* are in a very different vein. Here Nekrasov could indulge himself in broad irony and in caricature. Some of these poems are witty, but the wit is often grim and mordant. Soviet critics are tireless in stressing the importance of these satiric verses, but more for the attacks on czarist decadence than for artistic reasons. Over the years Nekrasov's basic techniques changed but little in his satiric poems. His original urge to caricature, and his fondness for grotesque exaggeration and distorting hyperbole remain nearly constant throughout his career. This does not mean, however, that he did not refine and polish his techniques, for he did sharpen his barbs and improve his attacks. But the fundamental approach remains the same and so do his favorite targets: the weaknesses of the aristocracy, the greed of the bourgeoisie, the brutality of the landowners, the officially cultivated hypocrisy of government officials at all levels, and as always the romanticizing, idealizing, and falsifying writers of the time.

The reader of a modern edition of Nekrasov's poems will find as the opening work, under the date 1845, the short "Contemporary Ode." The title itself is meant to be provocative, since it is clearly directed against the antique or idyllic themes of the Romantic epigones. As an ode it is a parody of the Classical ode, with just enough echoes of high style and serious tone to give a resonant background to the irony. With its satire of a "virtuous" man (actually, an exploiter), it belongs to the cycle of Nekrasov's Gogolian poems: the earlier "The Bureaucrat," "Cradle Song," and "Happy to See," and the later "A Moral Fellow" and "The Secret." All six poems are variations on a theme from Gogol, namely hypocrisy in the manner of Chichikov, the "hero" of *Dead Souls*. The first few lines are:

> You are adorned with virtues
> Which others are far from achieving,
> And—may heaven be my witness—
> I respect and esteem you deeply.
>
> You do not idly offend a cad,
> A villain even you are ready to help,
> And your rubles are never stolen
> From helpless widows and orphans.

Because the dishonest striving of an official was held up to scorn, the poem was highly praised by Belinsky. For the modern reader the advance over Nekrasov's earlier jingles and satires is hard to discover, although as usual Belinsky's opinion is shared by many

Soviet critics. They are fond of pointing out that one of Nekrasov's major contributions to Russian poetics is the innovation of using everyday speech and journalistic jargon in his satires.

The formula of censure in the form of ironic praise is a favorite with the young Nekrasov. When applied consistently throughout a poem, as it is in "Contemporary Ode," it means that every line must be understood in reverse, thus giving an effect of heavy-handed irony. The word "virtue" was at this period always used ironically by Nekrasov, who applied it only to scoundrels. Although the poem lacks the subtlety and refinements of satire to be found in his later works, there are other features besides the ironic formula which are characteristic of the poet at this stage and which point forward to more sophisticated verses. In a formal sense the three-syllable rhymes and the use of a three-syllable meter anticipate later, more significant poems. Most important is the apparent dialogue situation. The turn to the subject of the poem with the intimate form of address is a method of framing a poem which is characteristic of much of Nekrasov's poetry. The immediacy, directness, and suggested intimacy of many of his poems are owing to the voice the reader hears: the voice of the author, perhaps addressing someone as in his poem; the voice of a fictional figure of the poem; a dialogue; or even the poet's conversation with a child ("The Schoolboy"). The reader is always aware of a person behind the poem, and all that is described or narrated is passed through the prism of a personality.

In the same year he wrote the satiric "Cradle Song" in imitation of Lermontov's famous Cossack lullaby. The poem is clever in an unoriginal way. It is a parody of Lermontov's poem that is meant to satirize a corrupt official in the manner of our preceding poem. A rough translation of the first few lines will show how closely it resembles the original lullaby:

> Sleep, little rogue, while still harmless,
>   Lullaby.
> Dimly shines a copper moon
>   Upon your cradle.
> No fairy tale shall I tell you—
> 'Tis the truth I shall sing;
> Sleep then and close your eyes,
>   Lullaby.

This rather unsubtle satire called forth angry noises from the conservative press. The head of the *gendarmerie* wrote the Minister of National Enlightenment objecting to the poem. The censor who permitted the poem to be printed was reprimanded. Nekrasov, already a suspicious character in official circles, found himself enjoying unfavorable attention again. The informant-publicist F. Bulgarin wrote the Third Section that Nekrasov was a Communist who incited people to revolution, and he cited this poem as evidence. Even years later attacks on Nekrasov referred to this poem. The censorship prohibited publication of the poem in the second, third, and fourth editions of the poet's works. A lullaby for a corrupt official could raise a storm of such proportions in those days in Russia.

No more subtle and no different in style or technique is the short poem "A Moral Fellow" (1847) with its obviously ironic title. The poem is told by the moral fellow himself who reveals his hypocrisy and his failure as husband, father, friend, and serf-owner. Much more interesting is the longer "Hunting to Hounds" of 1846, written in the style of a comic epic. Here was a subject dear to Nekrasov's heart, for he was as passionate a hunter as Turgenev. In a light tone, with wit and comic effects, the poet makes fun of a favorite baronial pastime. Nekrasov is not a mere singer of sadness and sorrow, and it is misleading if amusing praise to call him the "bard of the proletariate." [6] The poem, which gallops along in dactylic hexameter, is a versified parody of two books on hunting, published in 1846. Both books praised hunting hares with hounds as a fine sport for owners of large estates and, while suggesting the snob appeal of the game, emphasized the esthetic qualities of hunting with dogs: "What is Beethoven to the sounds of the hounds!" They were humorless books written in pretentious, florid style, but on a theme dear to the poet's heart. In drawing the "hero" of the poem, Nekrasov introduced reminiscences of his own father. Much of the humor of the poem depends on the comic contrast between the magnificent equipment and grandiose martial maneuvers on the one hand, and on the other the object of the hunt—a bunny. "Death or victory" is the battle cry as the hunt sets out over hill and dale. The poet's own feelings are patently divided: in spite of the parodistic exaggerations and the reduction to the absurd, one can still hear the ring of genuine love for hunting, and this is what makes the poem still alive and interesting. The real theme of the poem, concealed under the fun and the baying of the hounds, is the problem of serfdom. The topic is introduced subtly and obliquely as early as the second line, which states that the "watchman yawns angrily," a remark criticized as absurd by Turgenev, but one which establishes immediately the relationship between serf and master. The hunter-serf-owner does not converse with his serfs, since he only yells orders at them, but he does talk with his dogs, whom he obviously values much higher. Because of fear of censorship, the poet does not expressly state the fact that a peasant's lamb was killed by the dog in the course of the hunt, and the peasant's angry threat to even the score was not printed until 1869.

There are other satiric poems which may still interest a modern reader. Interesting to students of Russian history is the poem "Excerpts from the Travel Notes of Count Garansky" (1853), which is a caricature of a Russian nobleman who has spent his life in western Europe but feels that he still knows intuitively how conditions are in Russia. He is a serf-owner, of course, a pompous and ignorant man who has never read a Russian book. Some of the satire suffers from being rather obvious. But the poem has some wit and the basic idea is a fruitful one. It was not printed in full, without censors' deletions, until 1922. As damningly characteristic of some aristocrats' knowledge of their own country the following lines are often quoted: "I also observed, from the window of my carriage,/ The life of the peasant: he is far from starving!"

III *Poems of Everyday Life*

In Nekrasov's *Verses* there is a type of poem which we shall call the poems on the drama of everyday life. These poems are vignettes of peasant life, often in narrative form, and usually set in a dialogue situation. One of the earliest of this type, and representative in nearly every respect, is "On the Road" (1845). The poem opens with the author requesting his driver to tell him something to dispel his boredom. The driver then tells how his wife, brought up tenderly in the home of an aristocrat, has suffered in her marriage to a peasant. Her upbringing has rendered her unfit for the hard work demanded of a peasant woman. The peasant driver tells the story in simple language, with rather naïve psychology kept within realistic bounds (he beats his wife only when drunk), and using not only popular turns of speech, but also dialect and regionalisms. The narrative, that is, the monologue of the cab-driver, is the poet's first attempt at reproducing popular speech. At the end of his brief tale the author thanks him for having diverted him, and they drive on. By framing the episode within a dialogue situation the poet locates it, makes it specific and visualizable, and invites the reader to share the experience. The theme of love and marriage was the only theme in the area of landowner-serf relations that could get by the censors. But the implications of the poem go far beyond the private sphere of personal relations and contain by suggestion an attack on the whole system of serfdom. The nobleman who sends an intelligent, sensitive girl out as a wife to a peasant thereby condemns her to a slow death. The caprice of the serf-owner is the direct cause of the young woman's ruin. This suggestion was not lost on those who were sympathetic to Nekrasov. It is in poems of this type that Nekrasov, continuing and enriching the heritage of earlier poets like Koltsov, made one of his important contributions.

Similar in language and in message is the poem "The Gardener," written in 1846. This is also the first imaginative work that firmly established Nekrasov in Belinsky's favorable opinion. It is told in the first person by the gardener, a handsome young fellow with whom a young aristocrat lady fell in love. When their affair was discovered by her parents, the young man was sent in chains to exile. The language is again that of popular speech, but with fewer dialect forms than in "On the Road." Nekrasov soon gave up all real regionalisms in his language. Only during the middle 1840's did he use them to any extent, and then only in poems where the central figure was a peasant. There are several stylistic borrowings from folk tales, notably the parallel negative clauses and the repetition of near synonyms. The poem is in many ways reminiscent of Koltsov's popular verses, but the note of class distinctions and their consequences is Nekrasov's own and owes nothing to any prototype. The censorship committee was divided on the question of permitting the poem, first published in 1846, to be printed in *Verses*. The last line and a half, spoken by the gardener more in resignation and acceptance of his fate, is: "Evidently it is not proper for a peasant-lout to love a nobleman's daughter." This statement, phrased in the prose of popular speech, has no overt anger or accusation, but it makes the message of the poem abundantly clear.

Much sharper, much more bitter are the later poems which describe the life and times of mid-century Russia. "The Forgotten Village," 1855, the next-to-the-last poem of *Verses,* is one of the bitterest. It is, at first glance, the description of the decay of a village forgotten by its aristocrat-owner, who only visits the village to be buried there. But the suggestion to those contemporaries whose ears were sensitive to such metaphorical implications was that the village was symbolic for Russia and for its condition of neglect and decay. As the day of the Peasant Reform drew nearer, Nekrasov's poems of everyday life became more caustic and revolutionary in tone. But throughout his career all the poems of this type had their barbs, and all of them, even apparently harmless ones such as "In the Village" or "On the Street" contain, even if hidden and indirect, their critical commentary on contemporary life in Russia.

Of all the Russian poets before Nekrasov, only Lermontov dealt with the theme of the fallen woman, and that only in a few poems. But this is a theme which Nekrasov turned to frequently in the 1840's. In 1845 he wrote "When out of the Dark," his first poem to have as the central figure a fallen woman. Since it was written in 1845, critics have usually assumed that the poet's personal experiences lie behind the poem. The voice of the author addresses the woman as he recounts her fate and their sharing of hard times. The woman is represented as a victim of sociological circumstances, a fact which endeared the poem to both Chernyshevsky and Dobroliubov. But the dominant note is not that of social criticism but rather of compassion and forgiveness: "I knew your story, child of misfortune!/And forgave it all and then forgot." "Whenever I drive at Night" (1847) has a first line which seems to echo Pushkin's poem, "Whenever I wander . . ." (*Brozhu li ia vdol' shumnikh ulits*), even to the dominance of the *u*-sound.

> Whenever I drive at night on darkened street,
> And storms are heard at dusk all day—
> O friend defenseless, ill and homeless,
> Before me suddenly your shadow gleams.

Told without pathos or sentimental effect is the tale of how the woman of the poem, apparently the author's mistress, offered herself as a prostitute to earn enough money to bury their dead child. This poem of compassion stirred Turgenev to the point of tears. As he wrote Belinsky, who was also deeply moved by it, the poem brought tears to the eyes of all who heard it when first read by the poet to the group at Mme Panayeva's home. It later became one of Chernyshevsky's favorite poems. Avdotia Panayeva, who in 1848 lost a son born to her and Nekrasov, was less impressed by the poet's pictures of fallen women and remained somewhat skeptical with regard to his sympathy with them, perhaps because she resented an autobiographical element in them. But the poem is personal or autobiographical only remotely, since it is rather the intertwining of the personal and social that is an innovation in Russian lyric poetry. It is also this interweaving of themes that makes it so difficult to assign such a poem to a particular genre. Important to Nekrasov is the compressed biography which explains the cause of the woman's fall from virtue. The dramatic form with its dialogue and intimate personal address are now familiar features that give the poem its peculiarly Nekrasovian flavor. The censors labeled the poem "immoral" and "harmful to religion." Again, as in "When out of the Dark," it is the voice of the author which addresses the woman with "thou" as he recalls their sharing of sorrow. The dactylic tetrameter has this time not the jingling rhythm of "Hunting to Hounds," but a solemn cadence evoking scenes of sadness and suffering. The first two lines contain the vowel *u* seven times, three of these under the accent. Four *o*-sounds in the same lines help lend a dark and foreboding tone to the opening words. In "Knight for an Hour" also *o*- and *u*-sounds predominate, for they are the favored sounds used to express the poet's gloom. This poem is evidence for a new and heightened use of the suggestibility of sound to reinforce meaning. Unusual for Nekrasov, who avoids heavy alliteration in the Germanic *Stabreim* manner, is the consonant alliteration of the third line, in which three of the four words begin with the letter *b*.

Not all of Nekrasov's poems on woman's fate are concerned with fallen women. There is a whole group of poems which are devoted to the lot of peasant women, to Avdotia Panayeva, and to the poet's mother. Several autobiographical poems also include references to his mother. One of the earliest poems concerned with the lot of peasant woman is the poem "Troika," which is addressed to a young peasant bride. The poem gives a double projection of the woman's future: at first a favorable prediction is made, as if the poet were entering into a part of the girl's wishes and wishful thinking. But the second part, more probable and realistic, makes a harsh and unhappy prophecy:

> From work both dull and exhausting
> You'll fade without blooming at all,
> You'll sink into sleep never ending,
> And only nurse and work and eat.
>
> Your face, so full of movement,
> So full of life—will suddenly show
> A look of dull endurance
> And senseless, constant fear.

In this vignette there is not a word of dialect or of popular speech, although the woman addressed is a peasant woman. The whole poem has the tonality of a folk song and a sustained cantabile quality. The song is Nekrasov's most appealing genre. Next in order is the tale in verse, a form which allows songlike parts. It is not to his satiric poems nor to his tendentious verses that we look for his greatest achievements. Except for details and minor techniques we cannot point to his development and growing maturity by referring to these categories.

Very similar, even to a prophecy of a hard and bitter life to come, is the poem "The Wedding," written much later in 1855. The author, a spectator at a peasant wedding, looks at the hopeful, expectant bride, and guessing her condition and her fears and hopes, finishes by predicting a fate like that of the woman in the earlier "Troika." Nekrasov was fascinated by the patient endurance of peasant women, but he was also embittered by it. Although he admired their courage and their spiritual and physical stamina, he objected to their lack of protest at their appalling condition, and nearly wept at the quiet submissiveness with which they suffered and endured.

The first and lasting model for all women who lead a life of silent suffering is the poet's mother. In the poem "The Fatherland," 1846, he said of her: "You feared to rise against your fate, Your lot you bore in slavish silence. . . ." "The Fatherland" is one of the earliest poems Nekrasov published which has a large confessional element. It is a bitter recalling of the poet's own youth, the sad figure of his mother, and the crude and brutal father. It stands in sharp contrast to the usual ecstatic tones of the contemporary patriotic hymns to Mother Russia. Written in rhymed six-foot iambs, it is one of Nekrasov's first successful poems in high style. Belinsky loved the poem, learned it by heart, and sent copies in his own hand to his friends in Moscow. The whole poem is suffused with the anguish of lost youth; even the poet's childhood nurse is recalled with bitterness. When first published in 1856 in *Verses,* it had to undergo several changes at the hands of the censors. The direct, personal pathos found an apposite form in a diction filled with abstractions and quite remote from the cantabile of the folk song which was Nekrasov's favorite. There are fewer concrete images and a generally more abstract, generalizing tendency than one usually associates with Nekrasov. *The Fatherland* is cast in a rhetorical form quite close to the style of his classicizing contemporaries. This is a manner of writing which he used only in poems of great pathos, such as "Elegy," "Muse," "A Terrible Year," "Russia," "Mother," and a few others. Throughout the whole period covered by the poems of *Verses,* iambic verse, often rhymed in couplets, is the preferred form for serious poems of this nature. This is the verse form perfected by Pushkin and Lermontov. When Nekrasov writes on lofty themes and resorts to abstractions and generalizations, he turns to a style reminiscent of theirs. Otherwise the three-syllable verse form, anapest and dactyl, are the measures he uses for poems nearer to folk songs, especially the songlike poems where he employs dactylic end rhymes.[7]

The poet's feeling of anger—a word of frequent occurrence—is the emotion which the poem communicates. The fictional occasion for the poem is a visit to his childhood home:

> And there they are again, familiar places,
> Where lived in idle, leisured luxury
> My forebears amid their mindless feasts
> And sullied, petty and perverted tyranny;

Verses: *The Harvest of a Dozen Years*

Where the swarm of trembling, suffering serfs
With envy eyed the life of hunting dogs,
Where I was destined to be born,
Where I did learn to tremble and to hate,
But keep my hate with shame well hidden,
For I was then serf-owner too . . .

Nine years later, in the poem "In the Fatherland" he wrote:

Ah, strangely I was formed by heaven's hand,
    And such my fate,
That bread from fields by serfs' hands tilled
    Could never nourish me.

IV *Avdotia Panayeva*

There is no separate cycle of poems dedicated to Avdotia Panayeva. Only occasional poems, scattered among his confessional lyrics—and these are not grouped by the poet either—can be identified as being addressed to her. Nekrasov tended to conceal intimate, personal feelings in this area either behind fictional characters or in generalized, typified experiences. Modern Soviet research has determined, for example, that the original occasion for "I Visited Your Grave" was not in fact death, but only temporary separation. Only in reworking and recasting the poem did it become a poem about death and final separation. The poet, in rewriting his poems, submerged and absorbed the original personal occasion and developed the theme of the poem in accordance with its own laws and artistic impetus, thereby obliterating most obvious autobiographical elements. By referrring to original manuscripts and to memoirs of intimate friends such as Chernyshevsky, recent Soviet scholarship has been able to reconstruct the occasion and the person addressed in many cases where a misunderstanding had continued for years. "In an Unknown Corner" was formerly assigned to his confessional lyrics, but recent research rediscovered his marginal notes to the poem and found his statement that it was an imitation of Lermontov and not personal in nature. The poem "A Heavy Cross Was Her Lot" was long considered to be addressed to his mother. Only on the basis of the testimony of Chernyshevsky has it been assigned to the poems addressed to Avdotia Panayeva. The poem is the severest self-indictment that Nekrasov ever wrote about his relations to Avdotia, his self-reproaches going to the point of hyperbole. Yet the purely autobiographical element was couched in such a way that it seemed reasonable to assign it to the poems about his mother.

The earliest poems to a beloved, "If, Tormented by Passion" (1847), and "You Are Always Good" (1847), combine requests for forgiveness with praise of the gentle kindness that sustains and soothes the poet. These two themes, namely the author's moody melancholy and the beloved's sweet forgiveness of his errors, reappear in many variations and modulations in nearly all the poems addressed to Avdotia. A naïvely biographical approach to these poems would reconstruct a long series of quarrels and misunderstandings, with hurt feeling on both sides, followed by scenes of reconciliation and renewed happiness. The general pattern is that the man (i.e., the author) has erred or given offense and now seeks reassurance and love once more from a beloved who soothes and comforts his troubled soul. Most of the poems are short, often written in trochaic tetrameter, with simple diction and rather conventional language. Even in the poem "Stricken by a Loss" (1848), which was occasioned by the death of their child, it is the woman's grief which is portrayed as being of primary concern. The two poems sent to Avdotia while she was abroad in 1850, "Yes, Our Life Together" and "Then it Was a Joke," emphasize his unhappiness at her departure, but do not ignore the theme of their difficulties when together.

But lovers' quarrels are not always treated pathetically and with conventional dramatic effects in his poems to Avdotia. In the poem "You and I are Muddled People" (1851), he exhorts his beloved to express her anger freely and not repress it. He had a fine sense for what he calls in this poem "the prose of love." Nekrasov knew very well that not all life could be summed up in a fine lyric cry and that everyday living did not consist only of ecstatic extremes of feeling. There is always with Nekrasov a final triumph of good sense and understanding, and return to reality and joy in things as they are. His poems to Avdotia in which this sense of reality prevails are the most charming and the least conventional. In another poem of the same year (1851), "O Letters of a Woman Dear to Us," he again successfully communicates both sensible understanding and genuine love. His poems to Avdotia are not original in the sense of new dimensions in love lyrics, but they have the ring of sincerity and deep feeling. The best of them illustrate the poet's ability to bring to life the little significant details that suggest in their new, personal context the feelings the poet wishes to express. In spite of the fact that shared grief and the poet's apologies are so prominent, a delicate intimacy and sense of belonging are suggestively evoked. The limits he set himself, the restraint in expressions of passion and longing, the ability to make magic out of everyday items—these features distinguish his love poetry and mark it as belonging to Nekrasov alone.

After 1855 the poet addresses no more poems to Avdotia. The years 1856 to 1857 were a time of crisis in their relations. Although the final break did not come until later, she seems not to have moved the poet to verse in their last years together. The children who were born to them all died in infancy. Most of their correspondence has been lost. Very revealing is a letter of the poet to Botkin in October, 1856 (X, 297). He regrets having made up with her again and says that he no longer feels that he needs her. Although he writes that he feels sorry for her, he also says of himself that he is weary of his constant sacrifices for her sake. When early in the 1860's their relationship formally came to an end, she disappeared completely from his writing.

V *Narrative Poems*

Many of Nekrasov's poems, such as "On the Road" or "The Gardener," tell a short story, and several of his early satiric poems have a thread of narrative; poems like "When out of the Dark" and "A Pretty Party" contain either a compact biography or a narrative element. But until the poem "Vlas" (1854) self-contained narrative, sustained as true storytelling, plays a minor role in Nekrasov's repertoire. For the future development of the poet, "Vlas" and "Sasha" are most fruitful for the later masterpieces such as "The Pedlars." "Red-nosed Frost" and "Russian Women" are anticipated by the style and compositional technique of these poems. According to Avdotia Panayeva's memoirs, "Vlas" was written after a long talk with a former serf of the poet's father. This serf had been drafted as a soldier, and after returning home had wandered about the country collecting money for the building of churches. Out of this oral material Nekrasov formed his famous poem of the rich peasant, who after years of sin and violence repents and in the garb of a penitent, girded about with chains, collects money from the country folk in order to build a church. The style is simple and direct and sparing with imagery and epithet. The lexical level is realistically kept within the range of a peasant, but there are neither dialect forms nor regionalisms. The poem is composed in folk-poem rhythms, that is, in both dactyls and trochees, but with the same number of accented syllables in each line. There are other characteristics of folk verse in the poem, such as the parallelisms in construction, sometimes contrasting in sense as in the following lines: "He walks in time of winter cold,/He walks in time of summer heat. . . ."

The poem made a strong but mixed impression on Dostoyevsky. In 1873, in the periodical *The Citizen,* he published an article taking issue with the poem, which he termed by and large a "comic" poem, although he conceded that there were beautiful passages in it. The figure of Makar Ivanovich of *A Raw Youth,* which he was writing in 1873, may have been influenced by the portrait of Vlas. In his *Diary* for that same year there is a tale entitled "Vlas," whose title at least may have been suggested by Nekrasov's poem. In his diary for 1877 Dostoyevsky mentions "Vlas" in a way which suggests that it was the zeal and great emotional drive of Vlas that impressed him most. Later in the same year he refers to the poem again: "Nekrasov, when he conceived his great *Vlas,* as a great artist, could not even imagine him otherwise than wearing chains, in repentant roving." [8] In the context of the quotation he emphasizes the fact that the repentant Vlas's actions are typical and represent a peculiarly Russian national trait.

Dostoyevsky's attention is drawn to the section of the poem after Vlas's miraculous conversion, but in its opening lines it is one of the very first poems in Russian literature which deals with a rich peasant's (*kulak*) exploitation of his poorer fellow peasants. The first part of the poem describes his robbing of his fellow men, his cruelty and lack of conscience. When it was first published in *The Contemporary* in 1855 it became well-known immediately, but was also at once subject to different views and interpretations. Some saw in it the tale of a conversion followed by exemplary piety. Others saw in it not just the story of sin, conversion, and rewarded piety, but also the severe indictment of a *kulak*. It is not a sentimental poem at all, for it documents with great realism a man's inhumanity to man, and it does not idealize the peasant or piously extol the alleged primitive virtues of an Orthodox *narod* in the manner of the Slavophils. Even the last lines of the poem may be interpreted in two ways. After describing how Vlas gathers in the widow's mite and the peasant's penny, the poet closes:

> Thus from the worker's mite
> Arise the churches of God
> On the face of our native land.

Thus churches are built through the pious generosity of the poor and humble; or thus churches are built with money taken from those who can least afford it.

In the poem "In an Unknown Corner" (1846) there is one of Nekrasov's earliest treatments of a theme of great importance in Russian literature during the whole early and middle nineteenth century, namely that of the "superfluous man." [9] The superfluous man is the leisured son of the artistocracy who has little learning, less ambition, and no real function in life. He is adrift in a world of whim and caprice, without responsibilities, plagued by his conscience in the best cases, leading a life of pleasure-seeking without goal or purpose and clouded by feelings of frustration and futility. Pushkin's Eugene Onegin belongs to this general class, of which Goncharov's Oblomov is perhaps the finest and most complete exemplar. Nekrasov's poem differs in some respects from the usual portrayal of the superfluous man, since it gives the reasons for the development of such a type and explains its origin as a result of the corrupting influence of serfdom and the disordered, capricious life of the serf-owners:

> In an unknown rustic region, in a half-wild village,
> I grew up among violent savages,
> And fate gave me, as a very great favor,
> Huntsmen as guides and tutors.
> Around me swarmed the debauchery of sordid licence
> And the struggles of senseless passion . . .

VI "*Sasha*"

Ten years later Nekrasov devoted the whole third section of *Verses* to the poem "Sasha," a longer narrative work that also treats the theme of the superfluous man in the figure of Aragin. What is new is the suggested connection between Aragin's being a superfluous man and the fact that he holds liberal views. This is the first time that a political note is added to the treatment of the theme. Chernyshevsky and Dobroliubov both considered the poem primarily an attack on the liberals, although of course they were not blind to other positive qualities of the poem. Aragin has often been termed an imitation of Turgenev's Rudin from the short novel of the same name, also published in 1856. Both works appeared in the same issue of *The Contemporary*. Nekrasov, however, had been working on his poem over a period of years, and had discussed it with Turgenev, so that the question of priority is an idle one. It is rather a case of remarkable affinity; the two friends produced similar characters contemporaneously. Aragin, an educated liberal, is blessed with the absolute inability to convert his convictions into deeds. Rudin, originally modeled on the character of M.A. Bakunin, is an intellectual of the 1840's. Aragin is a man of the 1850's, a serf-owner, and as a person much more negatively evaluated than Turgenev's Rudin. There are some possible literary echoes: Aragin's arrival in the village and his meeting with Sasha, the village girl who temporarily comes under his influence, reminds one of the meeting of Onegin and Tat'iana in Pushkin's *Eugene Onegin*. Sasha, although reminiscent of Tat'iana, is much closer to a Turgenev heroine, but this is not a matter of influence or imitation. In Turgenev's novels too it is often the woman who achieves in her life and actions what the man has only dreamed of as an ideal. The figure of Sasha is the literary predecessor if not the model of Liza in Turgenev's "A Nest of Noblemen," or Elena in *On the Eve,* and Vera Pavlova in Chernyshevsky's novel *What is to be done?* More important to us is the fact that she is the first of the series of great portraits of women which Nekrasov drew in the succeeding years.

The author is a person of the poem, and his voice, summoning and awakening, is the voice of conscience which clearly sets the accents and evaluations. It is his visits to the village and his conversations with Sasha's father which frame the story of Aragin and Sasha. The author's voice dominates the first, second, and fourth sections of the poem, especially clearly in the final section, in which Aragin's shallow resignation and weary renunciation of his ideals are related. The chapters told by the author in the first person are quite distinct in style and tone from the sections which give the inner narrative. The author's original emotion expressed is one of melancholy—not the modish Romantic melancholy of vague longing, but the appropriate feeling consonant with the sad pictures of village life and peasant problems. The meter is that of four-foot dactyls, up to Nekrasov's time a rare verse form in Russian literary poetry.

The poem, originally dedicated to Turgenev, was much liked by both Turgenev and other liberals like V. P. Botkin, as well as Slavophils like S. T. Aksakov. K. S. Aksakov and L. N. Tolstoy were pleased by the poem, because they thought it meant the end of Nekrasov's accusatory poems and pointed to his settling down to reconciliation with the state of affairs as it was then in Russia. They apparently missed the polemic slant of the poem, which is not to be found, of course, in the vivid and appealing evocations of nature, but in the revelation of the uselessness of a lazy intellectual. Aragin awakens Sasha's mind—his one positive contribution—but he accomplishes nothing himself and ends by renouncing as folly his earlier, lofty ideals and sinking back into a life of sloth and cynicism. At first Sasha is carried away by Aragin's eloquence and his high-minded talk about the "triumph of truth" and the brighter future to come. But she turns away from him when she discovers that these resonant phrases are mere chatter of an unrealistic kind and that Aragin intends to do nothing about them. In her first meeting with Aragin she is passive, a recipient, a listener and learner. But at the end she has become a person of action who puts into practice what Aragin had discussed so eloquently. She takes practical steps to help the peasants of her village, but her actions are only a beginning, as the poet reminds us in the oft-quoted lines: "Centuries will be needed, and blood and struggle,/In order to make men out of slaves." Sasha, for all the care the poet devoted to her picture, remains more a symbol than a sharply profiled person with individual traits. She stands for the younger generation, the young leaders of a future, better era. Nekrasov counted on his readers to see this and to hear the call to revolution ringing in the lines quoted above.

The liberals who overheard these tones still could find much in the poem of beauty and value that was not tainted with a revolutionary slant. The beauties of the Russian landscape, the charm of the changing seasons in field and forest, and peasant labor in sowing and reaping form the background for the growth of Sasha's awareness of life and its problems. Her thoughts and actions grow organically and in harmony with the processes of nature. Nekrasov characterizes Aragin and Sasha by their differing relationships to the climate and landscape of rural Russia. Aragin has no appreciation of it and contrasts it unfavorably with western Europe; Sasha has close spiritual ties with the soil of Russia and responds to it with love for its extent and its every detail.

The figure of Sasha represents Nekrasov's first portrayal of a "positive hero," a term intended as the antithesis of the superfluous man.[10] In time Nekrasov was to draw several heroes, but seldom without restraining realism and a sense of things as they actually were. In general he avoided the trap of overidealizing the popular tribune and preferred to portray the possibilities within the given historical context. Usually his tendency to idealize and draw over-lifesized figures is a part of his projection of the character into a better future. There is an exception to the general rule which should be considered in connection with the poem "Sasha." While the poet was in Italy and France in 1856 he worked on the long poem, "The Unfortunates," an unfinished narrative poem that was not published in *Verses*, but which is at once both a continuation of the theme of "Sasha" and a different, more tendentious approach to it. Krot, the central figure, is a somewhat idealized picture of a popular tribune, modeled in part on Belinsky. Krot is not a gentle village girl like Sasha, but an exile (in popular speech "unfortunate" meant political exile) who has been sent to prison for his revolutionary activities and specifically for his call for a popular uprising. The poem is divided into two parts, the first telling how the author was sent to prison for murdering his mistress. His early life, which contains many autobiographical details from Nekrasov's own youth in St. Petersburg, is described as one dedicated to private, selfish interests, thus preparing the contrast with the selfless devotion of Krot, which makes up the second part of the poem. Even in prison Krot is a leader of men, a guide and comforter who sustains the prisoners morally. At the end there is an ecstatic vision of Krot addressing a multitude and swaying them with the magic of his words.

There are several changes of style in the poem, which lacks cohesion in structure. The author's story is soon submerged in the description of Krot and is never completed. There is even some romanticizing in the rather unconvincing story of the author's love affair, and in places the pathetic tone leads to turgid rhetoric. Written in the Pushkin iambic form, it is one of his most Pushkinesque poems. A fragment at one time bore the subtitle "An Imitation of Pushkin" (II, 630). "The Unfortunates" represents a second, longer, and more revolutionary attempt to portray a positive hero. As a work of art the poem is a failure. With this exception, the later epic poems of Nekrasov are developments stemming directly from the narrative poems of *Verses*. The economy of the narrative poems gave him scope for delineations of nature and significant environment as well as opportunities for portraits of people. Historical observations, topical studies, the Russian landscape in its many moods, folk wisdom, the typical situations and attitudes of whole classes of people—these are some of the things which his poems now encompass and which are fruitful for the future.

VII *Personal Poems*

By no means all of Nekrasov's poems set forth arguments or plead a cause. Many of his personal poems only argue the thesis that he has failed as man and poet, or express his melancholy. "Bashfulness" (1852), for example, is a light and humorous poem about his awkwardness in society and his clumsy conduct in company. A more serious, almost bitter note is struck when he speaks of the years of deprivation in his youth and of the fact that he was afraid of his father. But the melody is not so somber and dejected as in the "Last Elegies," whose very title suggests the proximity of death. The elegies are intimate in subject, but partly formal in diction as they describe his condition of melancholy not only in abstract terms, but also with small, symptomatic, and sympathetic details, as for example the fact that his cigar no longer gives him comfort. (Dobroliubov wrote a parody on this.) In composition, the first elegy is interesting because of the unusual sustained metaphor of the imprudent traveler. For twelve lines the poet continues the image of the lost, confused wanderer who is finally taken to his grave. A figure of this type marks the poem as belonging to his rhetorical, pathetic style, so different from his usual verse with its concrete images that capture in a few words the essence of observed phenomena. When he felt that it was appropriate to his subject, the poet could use high flights of imagery and emotionally charged epithets. He could, when he chose to, command perfectly the language of the Romantics and achieve a Pushkin-like ring in his verse. His feelings of depression and dejection, the real subject of the "Last Elegies," were the substance of several poems in the early 1850's. His ill health and the end of the "dark years" contributed to the despondent and doleful tones that occur at this period. The words "severe," "stern," "despondent," "dejected," and "sad" become conspicuous in his vocabulary, suggesting a sense of deep melancholy and closeness to death as well as lending some of his poems their abstract quality.

"Life's Holiday—The Years of Youth" (1855) is a poem of self-derogation which not only laments his wasted youth but denies his skill as poet. He asserts that his poetry will not be remembered, because: "Free-flowing there is none in you,/My stern and clumsy verse!" The poem ends with the pathetic figure of the defenseless poet in a crown of thorns. It is one of his lesser efforts and interesting only for the depths of self-deprecation and self-pity to which he could sink.

In emphatic position as the last poem of *Verses* stands the poem "Be Silent, Muse of Vengeance and Sorrow!" It was written in 1855 at a time when he felt certain that he could not recover from his throat disease. With its iambic pentameter and its solemn tone of finality, it belongs among his poems of high style and pathos. If the famous first line (used also as title) is often quoted as being programmatic for all of his poetry, the last two lines are frequently referred to as his justification for his angry and accusatory poems: "That heart will not learn to love/Which has ceased to hate." This means that the last word of *Verses* is a verb "hate." Greater emphasis on the necessity of hating the evils of Russian mid-century society the poet could not achieve. With this last thrust the theme of his first collected verses returns to the program introduced by "Poet and Citizen" in more rhetorical and argumentative form, and in a simple, direct dictum defines the task of the poet as Nekrasov saw it.

CHAPTER 4

A Decade of Folklore and Satire: The Early Masterworks

From the yoke of enslavement
Deliver thy chosen people,
To whom the banner of enlightenment,
Lord God! thou hast entrusted in Russia.
(II, 260)

TO every poet nature gives only certain themes. There are subjects to which the poet will return again and again, for they are as much a part of him as his other hereditary traits. For every writer there are certain basic concerns which will be given form in various ways, modulated or even disguised, but they will make up the range of his subject matter. The situations, settings and plots will change, for they are the motifs, the part of his writing which is invented and which form, in the literal sense of motif, the motor power of his writing. But the themes will remain, for they are a given quantity. It is not surprising then that Nekrasov, returning to Russia after the success of his first book in much improved health, should continue to write on the same topics as before, even while inventing new motifs. For example, "Wretched and Modish" (1857) is again a poem on the fate of a fallen woman, but the intention of the poem is more to satirize her customers and competitors than to give a sympathetic view of her condition. Her story is, as the poet says, neither long nor new; in fact, it is a stereotype, a typical if unfortunate fate, contrasted with that of those who sell themselves for immediate gain and as a quick way to obtain a life of luxury. Here a note of sympathy is heard, but it is not primarily a poem of compassion like "Whenever I Drive at Night" or other earlier poems on the same subject. The tone of the poem is skeptical and satiric throughout, and belongs among his satires on contemporary life rather than among his poems of pity for the fate of women. Thus we can observe both continuity and change in Nekrasov's writing after 1856.

Travel in Europe restored not only his health but his perspective. His last longer effort as critic, the "Notes on Periodicals," occurs in this period of his life and represents a clarification of his theoretical views on literature. From Italy he brought back the idea of a comic-satiric supplement to *The Contemporary*, "The Whistle," but his outlet for wit and humor he soon turned over almost entirely to Dobroliubov. The poem which captures his mood of return to Russia is "Silence," 1857. His travel abroad seems to have reawakened his love for the Russian landscape as well as the need to express his relationship to it. His homecoming apparently aroused a renewed feeling of rapport with Russian literary tradition too, for the poem, written in Pushkin iambs, has many Pushkinisms and a formal style full of hyperboles and grandiose metaphors, especially frequent in pictures of distress and destruction. Perhaps for this reason it appealed to Ovsianikov-Kulikovski as "without doubt belonging to the best creations of Russian poetic literature." [1] In a letter to Turgenev of 25 December, 1857, Nekrasov writes that he composed the poem in part to mollify the censors and to show his loyal devotion as a subject of the czar, and it is true that he expresses his hope for better times after the Crimean War. In spite of this conciliatory intent, which may be taken with a grain of salt, the censors attacked the poem ruthlessly, and their changes and excisions made the original published version seem even more humbly devoted and czarist than Nekrasov could possibly have intended.

The title is to be understood as the peace and silence that came after the end of the Crimean War. The poem is divided into four sections. In the first the poet speaks of his love for his country, for the Russian landscape and people. Quite unexpected and most unusual are the references to his piety, the religious feelings aroused by the sight of a village church, and the mention of Christ in this first section. The village church is the arbitrary symbol chosen to represent the suffering of the *narod* during the war, but it is a strange choice of symbol for Nekrasov. The second section describes the country as it was during the Crimean War, noting the patriotism and the sacrifices borne by all levels of the population. The third returns to the countryside and its natural gifts, but also harks back to the war in describing the half-ruined Sevastopol. The final section reverts to the poet's impressions upon seeing his homeland again and being with its people. The basic theme then is the responses of the poet to his native country, and to its natural beauty and its fate in the hard years of the Crimean War and its aftermath. The poem combines ardent patriotism with subjective lyricism, giving a fitting expression to his reidentification with Russia after the months abroad.

The poem is considered one of his most "liberal" poems, and it is true that the reunion with his beloved Russia evoked milder tones than many which we have heard in *Verses.* But if we compare the picture drawn by Nekrasov with some typical positions taken by liberals in the late 1850's, we shall see that Nekrasov was still far from the attitudes of the really convinced liberals. In 1856 V. I. Dal warned against the introduction of general literacy and its harmful effects in a letter to the periodical *Russian Discussion,* and in the same year defended the patriarchal nature of the relationship of landowner to serfs.[2] As late as 1857, only four years before the emancipation of the serfs, Davydov came out in favor of corporal punishment for serfs. The position of the more moderate liberals was that serfdom had to be abolished, but somehow without changing things fundamentally, and they hoped for great things to come from the modest, moderate changes to be instituted under the kind rule of a beneficent czar. Obviously not all their hopes were realized, but they continued their optimistic attitude in the face of the peasant revolts and other drastic dislocations in Russian society following the emancipation.

I *Poems of the* Narod

The state of the *narod* continues to be uppermost in the poet's mind. In 1857 for the first time he wrote a poem dealing directly with the peasant revolts, "The Riot," a brief sketch of the bloody pacification of a peasant uprising in the province of Riazan. In 1876 the poet tried unsuccessfully to get the fragment past the censors, and the poem was not published until 1913. More significant is the longer portrait drawn in the same year under the title "Reflections at the Mansion Door," usually dated 1858. In a prosy beginning ("There is the mansion door. On festival days . . .")

appropriate to the sarcastic satire of the opening lines, he describes the main entrance to a mansion, guarded by a doorkeeper in uniform who turns away petitioners. A group of humble peasants comes, waits respectfully, is refused audience for its grievances, and goes away peacefully and without protest. The picture of class conflict leads the poet to reflect on the lot of the *narod*, exposed to the whims of its oppressors, who lead lives of leisure and luxury without regard for anything but their own pleasure. Famous are the lines:

> Go to the Volga: whose moan is heard
> Over the great Russian river?
> This groan we call a song—
> The boatmen tug their tow-line . . .
> Volga! Volga! In your spring flood
> You do not fill the fields so full
> As our native land overflows
> With the people's great sorrow.

Five times in the last fourteen lines the word *ston* (moan, groan) is repeated. The poem proceeds from a description of the petitioners at the entrance to a mansion, to satire with rhetorical questions addressed to the indifferent gentry, and finally to the state of the nation at large, the *narod* and its suffering. The starting point of the poem, as so often with Nekrasov, is the poet's observation of a scene from daily life. Typical is not only the visual basis for the point of departure, but also the short narrative precisely placed in the environment described.

"Reflections" was first printed in Herzen's *The Bell* in London in 1860,[3] and soon became famous throughout Russia, especially the lines just quoted. The first lines translated above have a vowel harmony based on the vowels *o* and *a:*

> *Volga! Volga! vesnoi mnogovodnoi*
> *Ty ne tak zalivayesh' polia*
> *Kak velikoyu skorb'iu narodnoi*
> *Perepolnilas' nasha zemlia.*

The line following those translated above starts with a short, aphoristic formulation: "Gde narod, tam i ston": "where the *narod* is, there is also a groan." Such an interruption marks the poem as belonging to his didactic style. His style and tone vary, however, not just in each section, but almost from line to line. Nekrasov now commands such a wealth of nuance that he is able to change his diction without the transition being felt as a break in style, because both the sense and the sustained onward thrust of the verse carry the reader along. The final section, which ends in magnificent song, starts with a deliberate prosaism: "However, why bother such a big shot for the sake of little people?" The poem is difficult to classify, because it has an ode, an elegy, a descriptive section, and political invective. The style varies from the high rhetoric of the ode to the prosiness of the descriptive part, with melodic sections at the end, and throughout are heard echoes of the language of the satiric vaudeville. It is reasonable to remark that the first part of the poem is narrative, the second satirical, and the third lyrical or subjective; but the important achievement of the work in respect to its art is that the poet has succeeded in making an entity and artistic unit out of the dissimilar parts. Throughout the poem the perspective of the poet—an emotionally involved spectator—is preserved, and the poet's own participation is a unifying factor amid the diverse styles.

One of Dobroliubov's favorite poems was "A Song for Erema" (1859). The poem had a very wide circulation during the 1860's, because it became the adopted song of the young revolutionaries. Dobroliubov memorized it and sent copies to friends, urging them to learn it by heart too. The poem was understood by its contemporary readers—those who were alert for such things—as a clear summons to revolution. In *The Contemporary* at this period the names Foma and Erema, common names from folk tales, were used for peasants who were servile and did not protest but submitted ignorantly and passively to the whims of the landowners. Such peasants were a source of irritation to Nekrasov and the radicals. Nekrasov was not blind to the differences among peasants. Those who were household serfs, those who were *kulaks* or in some way lived at the expense of their fellow peasants, and those who strove to emulate their masters were heartily disliked by the poet. His best-liked class of peasant, and the one most frequently mentioned, is the ploughman, the worker in the fields. As a figure of the poem, Erema is a peasant child whose future is still undetermined; he is only a type, not an individual, and is presented as a symbol of the immaturity of the peasant masses.

The meter is that of four-foot trochees, with the odd lines having dactylic end-rhyme. Russian folk poetry has a generally trochaic cadence, often ending the line with a dactyl; dactyls may often replace trochees in the middle of the line also. In structure the poem reminds the reader of the early short narrative poems, framed by dialogue, that Nekrasov wrote in the 1840's: "On the Road," "The Gardener," and others. The first lines, which consist of the author's address to his driver, are strongly reminiscent of the opening lines of "On the Road." The author enters into conversation with a village nurse, who sings to a child while the parents are busy with the harvest. She advises him to strive for personal happiness in the light of traditional wisdom. The author then addresses the child, giving quite the opposite advice: the meaning of life is not to be found by following traditional experience, namely that kind of folk wisdom which recommends emulating the gentry and seeking to attain station among them, but on the contrary it lies in service to the *narod* and in struggling for Brotherhood, Equality, and Freedom. The child is admonished to scorn the servile endurance of wrong and to turn against his oppressors; most of the verbs in the part spoken by the author are in the form of the imperative. (Even Dobroliubov admitted that it was a didactic poem.) Remembering the last word of *Verses*, the reader is not surprised when the author counsels "Unbridled, savage enmity for oppressors" and links "this righteous hatred" with "the sacred faith." The ring of these lines is unmistakable, for they have the genuine tenor of Nekrasovian hate. The poem ends by returning to the dialogue frame: the child awakes, is taken by the nurse, and the nurse continues to soothe him by singing her song.

In 1861, the year of the emancipation of the serfs, there were 1,176 peasant uprisings. This is the figure released by the government, not necessarily the actual count. Nekrasov, as we already know, officially ignored the emancipation, and *The Contemporary* treated it with the silent contempt that seemed its due. There are, however, several poems which were directly prompted by the freeing of the serfs and the resulting unrest, among them "Freedom" (1861), "Hardly a Year" (1861), and "On the Death of Shevchenko" (1861). Throughout the poet's career his poetry reflected current events, but at this time of troubles all his poems are deeply influenced in some way by the changes in Russian society that were taking place so rapidly. "Freedom" was not printed until 1869; in 1861 there would have been no possibility of slipping it past the censors. Often quoted are the lines: "I know: instead of the snares of serfdom/They've now invented plenty of others. . . ."

The death of the great Ukrainian poet of freedom, Shevchenko, who had been very close to the staff of *The Contemporary* after his return from exile, called forth one of the bitterest poems of this group. Although there are no direct and open references to the emancipation, the topic makes itself felt through the harsh irony so that it may be called a cryptic theme of the poem. The problem of unemployment that arose immediately after the freeing of the serfs and the dislocations in the labor market are the subject of the poem "Meditation" (1861). In 1860 the poet wrote a purely personal poem of regret at the loss of Turgenev from the circle of his friends, without reproaches or bitterness. "Alone, Lost" is a sad poem, a poem of the recall of happier days. The fourth line reads: "D*u*shu rodn*u*yu moy*u*," one of many examples of Nekrasov's use of vowel harmony with the "sad" vowel *u*. The fourth quatrain contains a line unusual for its cluster of hushing consonants: "Ty eshchë zhazhdesh' i zhdësh'." "For Turgenev," not published until 1913, was considered for a long time to be addressed to Herzen. The person addressed in the poem is a former companion and co-worker who turned liberal on the eve of the emancipation. The poem is a sharp polemic, especially since the former friendship and understanding is contrasted with the present loss of idealism. The poet reproaches his former friend for the abandonment of his earlier critical attitude and for the desire to see a real "dawn" rather than a "doubtful ray of light" in the freeing of the serfs. The difference in tone between the two poems to Turgenev is due not primarily to their personal dissension, but to their differences in attitude to the peasant question.

II *Children's Poems*

The lot of peasant children in the middle of the century was naturally strongly influenced by the increasing industrialization of Russia. Child labor in the factories is the subject of Nekrasov's poem of pity, "The Children's Tears" (1860). The whirring of the factory wheels and the constant, relentless demands of the machines are suggested by onomatopoeic effects and repetitions:

Khot' umri—prokliatoe vertitsia,
Khot' umri—gudit—gudit—gudit!

A year later he returned to a theme close to his heart and nearer to his own experience than city factories: "Peasant Children" (1861). In a formal sense too the poem is familiar, since it is again narrative in nature, and the author is an active person in the poem. Autobiographical elements are interwoven with descriptions of contemporary rural life—a favorite feature of a Nekrasov poem. The opening lines function as an introduction, telling of the author-hunter's rest in a barn, during which he overhears village children talking about him as they watch him. The second, main section of the poem contains reminiscences of the poet's own youth, much of which was spent in play with peasant children. There are several lyric digressions, one of which, about the child Vlas, is of considerable length and is remarkable for its pathetic intensity. This part, beginning "Once, in the cold winter time . . . ," has been learned by heart by generations of school children in Russia. Often referred to in this same section is the passage in which the six-year-old Vlas asserts confidently that there are two men in the family: himself and his father. (Two men for the work to be done.) There is a special charm in all the poems in which Nekrasov reproduces conversations with children. He had a fine ear for the living language of children and peasants, and was able to represent it in its effect without condescension or even seeming to simplify.

III *Peasant Poems and Folklore*

The cycle of Nekrasov's peasant poems would not be complete without mentioning poems like "The Green Sound" (1862), "Kalistrat" (1863), and "Songs" (1866).[4] All the poems referred to are strongly influenced by Nekrasov's growing interest in folklore. His youth was spent in contact with living folklore, and his mature years in the formal study of it. During the 1850's and early 1860's publications of folkloristic information and collections of folk tales and poems formed a significant section in *The Contemporary*. Both camps—Slavophils and the revolutionary democrats—were busy collecting, editing, and publishing folklore from all corners of Russia. The title itself, "The Green Sound," comes from a Ukrainian folk song and means the spring of the year. The poet introduced several echoes of folklore into the poem, which sings of nature's seasons of winter and spring, spring being the time of reconciliation. The poem is told in the voice of a deceived husband, whose varying responses are narrated in harmony with the change of seasons. Throughout the years it has remained one of Nekrasov's most popular poems. It is the first poem written by the poet in unrhymed three-foot iambic lines, the verse form which he used later with such flexibility and elegance in "Who Can Be Happy in Russia?" For a poem about peasants it is remarkably light and cheerful. But, of course, the poverty and misery of the peasants are not the sole subject of his verse, for he was also fascinated by the sense of humor the peasants preserved and the irony with which they could view their own situation. "Kalistrat" captures this mood of cheerfulness and mild irony perfectly. "Matchmaker and Groom" (from "Songs") is also a light, humorous poem —Nekrasov knew well the customs of the peasants and their ability to take life humorously when opportunity offered. For poems of this type which deal with peasant customs, Nekrasov usually chose the folk-song trochaic verse, using it with considerable freedom in either four- or six-foot lines. In the song the poet is always at ease and natural, the lines flow freely and musically, and effortlessly produce a cantabile effect. It is not surprising then that many of his poems have become folk songs and passed into the oral heritage of folk poetry.

Nekrasov always used critically material drawn from folk sources; not all folk tales were apposite to his purpose. The collections of folk tales and proverbs published during the 1850's and 1860's were, like everything else that appeared in print, subject to censorship. Deleted from the collections was everything that seemed critical of or harmful to the state and the established religion and its clergy. Thus tales at the expense of the village *pop* (priest), for example, were suppressed, although everyone knew that there were many such tales. Quite naturally Nekrasov had mixed feelings about the folkloristic collections of the Slavophils, whom he correctly suspected of editing their works to suit their own purposes. But he followed research in the field of folklore very carefully. He knew V. I. Dal's *Proverbs of the Russian People* (Moscow, 1862) in manuscript before it was published. In the early 1860's several collections of A. Afanasev were familiar to him as were also I. Khudiakov's and A. Erlenveyn's collections of fairy tales (*skazki*). Even earlier A. Pypin had published in 1856 in *Notes of the Fatherland* his "Fairy Tales of the Russian Nation." The poet's critical judgments on this material were tempered by his own personal familiarity with folk customs and by his desire to present peasant life with his own slant. Therefore he deliberately adapted his sources to what he wished to communicate.

An example of his reworking of a folklore source may be observed in the poet "Katerina" from the cycle "Songs" (1866).[5] An old folk song "Come in, Sun" tells how a young peasant wife not only submits to the will of her in-laws, but obeys them cheerfully and prides herself on her patience. The poem counsels submission and obedience as prime virtues. It was reprinted in "Russian Conversation" in 1856 as evidence for the peasants' natural tendency to obey and submit and their pleasure in giving in to the will of others. Nekrasov reversed the sense of the poem and converted it into an attack on such docile behavior; the poem is at first glance a poem of protest against the despotism of the in-laws, but in a larger sense it is also a protest both against the capricious oppression of peasants in general and the servile spirit of submission which the poet so disliked. "What the Old Woman Thinks" (1862) is another poem with a similar corrective tendency. The old woman, unable to sleep at night, recalls her life of "sin." The theme of the poem is the relaxed, almost defiant attitude of the peasant woman to what is generally considered to be sin. She is not afraid of sin; on the contrary, she recalls her strayings from the path of virtue with pleasure. She does not repent or really feel regret but has a rather unworried attitude toward her adventures, some of which are rather trivial. At the same time the force of custom and training is strong; the poem's ending contains the traditional words of confession of sin and a plea for intercession. But if one carries through to the final words the basic tone of the poem, then the ending is mildly ironic. The poem need not, however, be interpreted as a cryptic attack on religion; it is rather a realistic assessment of peasant piety, which often contains behind the religious postures and formulas a vigorous joy in life unaffected by theology. In the same year he wrote the poem "At the Height of the Harvest," which describes the hard labor demanded of peasant women. The tendency here too is to correct the idyllic pictures of village work which were put forth by those who saw the institution of serfdom as an ideal ordering of society. His description of a peasant woman at work includes details like the sting of flies and the sweat and weariness of hard work in the fields. There was a definite polemic purpose behind Nekrasov's realistic pictures of peasant life. For the modern reader uninterested in righting ancient wrongs, there remain skillfully drawn and interesting portraits of a bygone era.

Nekrasov recast the proverbs, folk turns of phrase, and all forms of material from folk sources before using them in his poems. Very few unaltered quotations can be found in his verse. His most common procedure, where he did not also alter the sense, was to shorten the original and make it more concise. In some of his poems in the 1840's he had been content to use folk-song clichés: if speaking of lips, then they must be red; if of a girl, then she was inevitably pretty or beautiful; if of cheeks, then full and red; teeth were always white. Standing epithets, often repeated, are characteristic of the Russian folk song. But most of these epithets become empty, are not specific and do not individualize. In the 1860's the poet avoids them for the most part. There are a few in "Red-nosed Frost," but in general Nekrasov achieved the effect of folk song with a vocabulary that was either literary or approximated the literary standard.

Such stylistic changes, usually in the direction of greater precision, went along hand in hand with his didactic, propagandizing alterations. Dobroliubov and Chernyshevsky consistently called for critical attention to contemporary living conditions, especially to the economic conditions of the peasantry. For them folklore and studies in ethnography were not academic studies but the raw material for propaganda purposes. They were not content with writing which merely described conditions, but demanded that the writers of the time should show the causes behind the state of affairs. Their theories had a great influence on Nekrasov's use of popular speech and folklore in the late 1850's and early 1860's. The poet had only one really important predecessor in this field. Kolstov had written successfully on rustic themes, and many of his poems even bore the stamp of Belinsky's approval. Nekrasov's early poems, such as "The Gardener" or "On the Road" owe much to Koltsov's earlier poems on similar subjects. Nekrasov followed him in adopting in his language several turns of speech, the use of standard epithets, the repetition of near synonyms, and to a degree the vocabulary of folk poetry with its dialect. But the poet could also write poems about peasant conditions with criticism of social injustice without using the lexicon of popular speech: "Muse," "In the Fatherland," "The Forgotten Village," and "Silence," to mention a few examples. There is a strong accusatory element in all of these works, but the style and vocabulary are not strongly influenced by folk poetry.

Many other writers in the 1860's were writing about the social scene in Russia. Under the influence of Dobroliubov and Chernyshevsky, *The Contemporary* ran a whole series of articles, reports, travelogues, and essays describing the vast Russian lands. Ethnographic studies now began to appear in great numbers. Saltykov-Shchedrin, N. V. Uspensky, and V. A. Sleptsov are among those who wrote articles, many of them very critical of the backwardness of the lower classes all over Russia. The ignorance and superstition of many sections of society were described in unprettified terms. Even many of the traditional peasant rituals, customs, and forms of living, formerly viewed as quaint if noticed at all, were now depicted as merely backward and at best suspect and in need of enlightenment. Thus it came about that some peasant customs, formerly considered colorful expressions of the folk spirit, such as wedding feasts or lamentations for the dead, were now often looked at suspiciously by some of the more dedicated apostles of enlightenment. Nekrasov did not go to such extremes, but he was well aware of this attitude toward folkways and therefore not only selected his material very carefully but also wove it into the fabric of his poems with an eye to the effect on readers of the intelligentsia.

Only in two poems of the 1860's does the poet himself speak directly to the reader about the condition of the peasants: "The Site of the Fire" (1863) and "At the Height of the Harvest." In all the others he lets the peasants speak for themselves and their lot in life. Yet the presence of the author is felt in all these latter poems too, especially in "Orina, the Soldier's Mother." In some poems, such as "Village News," there are colloquial words, and some of the language is a modified form of popular speech. Where there was a choice of near synonyms, Nekrasov often chose the word appropriate to folk language, but still acceptable and understandable in the literary language. But in general the impression of popular speech is attained by the use of questions, direct address in the familiar dialogue situation, and exclamations and other conversational turns. In cases where Nekrasov adopts the traditional form of a lamentation, he usually makes the general phrases of the mourning formulas more precise, enumerating the specific accomplishments of the deceased rather than using the stereotyped phrases. In "Red-nosed Frost," however, he gives both the traditional form and his own more exact modification of a lamentation. New and unusual in Nekrasov is the successful combination of the song form and its rhythm with the vocabulary and intonations of conversational speech, often with hardly perceptible transitions.

The poet's sister, A. A. Butkevich, reports that a certain peasant woman Orina told her story to Nekrasov, who then used her narrative as the basis of "Orina, the Soldier's Mother" (1863). The poem is introduced in a fashion now familiar to the reader: the poet returns at night from the hunt to seek shelter for the night with Orina. In the conversation that develops she tells how her strong son returned from military duty broken in body by the harsh and inhuman treatment he received in service. His spirit and willingness to work are emphasized by mother Orina, who tells of his joy in working as a youth. But after his return from military duty only the will to work is left; the young man's health has been ruined, and he soon dies. When the mother grows silent, remembering her sorrow, the author continues with his questions, thereby leading her on to tell more. The presence of the author in the poem has its familiar function: his feelings and attitudes, expressed by his sympathetic questions, set the accents and suggest the evaluations. Thus in the intimate dialogue situation the mother's restraint in telling of her own and her son's suffering and her glowing enthusiasm when speaking of his virtues become a severe indictment of the cruelty of military service.[6] It is in fact more the poet than the mother who expresses feelings of sorrow and sympathy; the mother's narrative is simple, understated, and so restrained that it underscores all the more effectively the tragedy of her son's ruined life. The language is full of popular turns of speech, and there are many folkloristic elements in the poem. But almost all of them are actually not borrowings, but Nekrasov's own reworking or adaptations of peasant language, especially the tones of the lamentation. In the 116 lines there are 30 caressing diminutives used, many of them in end rhyme.

IV *"The Pedlars"*

The early 1860's mark a turning point in Nekrasov's poetry from poems about the *narod* to poems of and for the *narod.* The first of these, the famous "The Pedlars" (1861), is dedicated to a peasant who had been a hunting companion of the poet, Gavril Iakovlevich Zakharov. In the dedication the poet expresses his hope that the peasant will be pleased by the poem. Not only Zakharov was pleased by the poem: parts soon became folk songs, widely spread and memorized, and during the lifetime of the poet it was among the very best known of his poems. Over the years the poem's appeal has been greater than that of some of his more mature works; Mirsky, who considers the masterpiece "Russian Women" to be a "mechanical paraphrase," admired "The Pedlars." [7] The motif is again that of travel, that is, the wanderings of the pedlars. There is also a brief and charming love story in the first part; but it is not completed, and at the end the reader loses sight of the bereft girl and hears only of the fate of the pedlars. With its greater length compared with an earlier narrative poem such as "Sasha" it affords the poet room both for more detailed descriptions and longer lyric interludes. While the poem is primarily a narrative, the verse form and the tonality are songlike throughout, so that it might be classified as a "song" that has been extended to epic dimensions. The dactylic rhymes underline the folk-song nature of the verses. Often the beginning of a line is anapaestic (instead of the expected trochee), so that the dancing movement of the generally four-foot trochaic lines is interrupted, and the metrical freedom of the song is approximated. As is usual in Nekrasov's poems of this type there are frequent diminutives in *-ushko,*

-iushko or *-enko,* and they are favorites in the end rhymes. It should be noted, however, that many of these words ending in the diminutive suffix are not necessarily "caressing diminutives" or terms of affection; many are merely conventional and devoid of any particular expressiveness.

Diminutives are not the only forms which Nekrasov uses in order to lengthen the word to obtain a dactylic foot. The urge to "dactylize," if we may coin a word, is so strong, that often the expected, normal word is extended by some means, if a noun then by a suffix. There are also many verbs extended either by attaching a prefix—or even two—or by using the frequentative form of the verb, which usually spreads the word by infix and moves the accent back. The words so lengthened are by no means distorted; the use of prefixes often means greater precision in meaning, and the use of the frequentatives helps lend folk-song quality to the lines while staying within the lexical limits of the literary language. Even the syntax is kept simple and within the range of folk speech. Many single lines form a complete and independent syntactical unit by themselves. Caesuras are infrequent, so that the lines tend to flow without interruption. Enjambment is rare, so that when the syntactic unit is spread over two lines, the first frequently ends in a comma or natural pause. If the sentence is carried over four lines, which is infrequent, then the unit generally breaks up naturally into two equal and semi-independent groups of two lines each. The same techniques we have noted before are applied here too, namely the repetitions of words, sometimes even in the same line, parallelisms and repetitions of either whole phrases or a phrase and its nearly synonymous equivalent, and the use of doublets in verbal phrases: "goes-walks." These are all stylistic features of the narrative-descriptive sections, but in addition there is an interpolation, Tikhon's "Song of the Poor Wanderer," which is pure song.

The poem is divided into six main sections. The first is a lyric introduction, describing the love between Katia and Van'ka, the younger of the two pedlars. There is both delicacy and realism in this well-known love scene. Unselfish, genuine love is portrayed, but the theme of the pedlars is one of trade, so that the language used is that of trade transaction; humorously and gently the poet uses a kind of peasant Aesopian language to express indirectly their love for each other; only later, in the third section, does he depict Katia's faithfulness and her hopes and love. The second section is devoted entirely to a description of the bargaining that the pedlars carry on in the village. The pedlars naturally are trying to make as much money as possible, and Tikhon, the older of the two, is portrayed here as greedy and eager to take advantage. Yet the total picture is by no means unsympathetic, since the pedlars are peasants too, and as much members of the *narod* as the people with whom they are dealing. The third and fourth sections extend the picture of the second, adding references to real exploiters in the village: not only the aristocratic serf-owners, but also the bourgeoisie, which is growing and expanding at the expense of both the peasants and the landowners. The greed of the merchant class and the growing impoverishment of the old aristocracy are given their due in the fourth section. The fifth is devoted entirely to the love theme, that is, to Katia's longing for her lover and to her labors as she waits for him to return. The final part turns again to the narrative of the adventures of the pedlars up to their tragic end. There are two digressions from the story of how the woodsman kills the pedlars then meets his own end. One, the song of the poor wanderer, has already been mentioned. It is monotonous, partly because of the long refrains, harmonizing with the harsh conditions of life for the peasants. Hunger and cold drive the peasants into savagery and drunken debauchery. The other digression is the story of Titushka the tailor, which combines with the song of the poor wanderer to give by implication a strong revolutionary tendency to the final section: the passive subservience of the peasants must come to an end.

In form, style, and narrative technique "The Pedlars" represents a completely new departure in the literary verse of its day. It is the first poem which satisfies the demand of Dobroliubov that the new poetry should be of and for the *narod,* and not just written about the *narod* for the delectation of the intelligentsia.[8] To ensure the wider dissemination of the poem, Nekrasov had it printed in 1862 in cheap brochures which sold at three kopecks apiece. He took no profit from the sale of these for himself but financed the project entirely from his private funds. A second issue of the inexpensive pamphlets was made before the government prohibited further printing. To students of the poet who have followed his development this far, the innovational quality of the poem may seem minimal, but it is striking if one considers what the other contemporary writers of the period were producing. The early 1860's are a time of the consolidation of "pure poetry," whose theorists Fet, A. K. Tolstoy, and Maikov were opposed to all forms of didacticism or tendentiousness in poetry. In addition they wrote for a small, elite audience. Fet especially was offended by Nekrasov's urge to write for the masses. Nekrasov was clearly in opposition to such elitist theories of literature, but he was also equally critical of dilettantes in the field of "popular" writing. Quite early in his career he wrote polemically against those pseudopopular poets who tried to write "folk literature" simply by avoiding the language they would normally use for educated people and substituting regionalisms and tag-ends of dialect.[9] By "poetry for the people" in the Dobroliubov sense Nekrasov meant poetry which literate peasants—there were such people in the 1860's—could read and understand. At the same time this poetry should also satisfy the canons of esthetics and the artistic requirements of the intelligentsia. His formula for such poetry was: simple form and language with a profound content. Thus in "The Pedlars" he tells a very simple, straightforward tale, but the content of the poem and its implications are much richer and deeper than any retelling of the plot would suggest.

The plot comes to an end when the woodsman, who has brutally murdered the two pedlars for their money, is taken away to prison. This crime of violence in a folk tale is not due to a specific model that Nekrasov was following, nor to a desire for dramatic violence in the poem. Rather it is a glaring example of a totally destitute man committing a crime against his fellow paupers, and the drastic nature of the incident is intended to underline a message. Dobroliubov had stated that crime is the result "not of the nature of a man, but the consequence of his being placed in an abnormal relationship to society." Therefore the woodsman is shown as not innately evil but as a product of dire poverty and unjust social conditions. Emphasis is given to his odd and poor clothes, for example. In addition to being the product of bitter ignorance and deprivation, he is also simple to the point of being simple-minded. Nekrasov's interest in portraying him this way is evidenced by the fact that the love story of Van'ka and Katia is forgotten at the end for the sake of the ending the way it is: with the officials, in all probability, taking the money stolen from the pedlars and leading the poor and stupid woodsman to jail.

The peasant movement was the great force and the pressing issue of the day. Nekrasov intended the poem to be topical but without being obviously tendentious. In view of the fact that the poem was intended to be read by peasants, it is interesting to note that in the days of the emancipation literate peasants were in great demand to read and explain the edict of emancipation to their illiterate fellow peasants—the great majority of peasants. Those who could read often gave quite fanciful interpretations, distorted much, and thereby caused great confusion, disillusionment, and a sense of uncertainty. The result was that the peasants felt that they had been deceived and betrayed; some believed that the czar had meant well, but that the officials had corrupted his message of deliverance. False prophets arose with messianic messages, some of them pure charlatans, some simple victims of ignorant misunderstandings. Whole villages were set in motion by these people, and migrations took place which dislocated the village life of whole provinces. Some of those who started to wander were only seeking work ("Meditation," "Kalistrat"), but others were looking for the free land allegedly promised by the czar, or believed that they were marching for some vague cause, or simply were starving and seeking food. The poem is addressed to this situation of uprisings, unrest, violence, and their resulting repression in two ways. The opening part of the poem describes in charming pictures the state of happiness, hope, and cheerfulness of which peasants are capable in ordered circumstances; the ending demonstrates the possibilities for anarchy and crime which result directly from ignorance and superstition. But this moral lesson, if indeed it is appropriate to derive one at all, is not obtrusive; the poem lacks the didactic tone which we have noted in other poems of Nekrasov. The narrative is told without commentary and without preaching, and the songlike nature of the verse carries the reader forward with its cajoling melody in such a way that there need be little thought of propaganda.

To avoid misunderstandings among peasants as well as among educated people, Nekrasov added footnotes to the poem explaining the few words of dialect origin which he used (II, 142). Many proverbs and folk sayings are woven into the text. Sometimes the poet felt the necessity of explaining them, especially when they were allusive. Some of the folklore in the poem has its origin in the poet's home district of Iaroslavl'. The town of Poshekhon'e, for example, is known for simple-mindedness in folk tales of the region. Popular songs are echoed, some of them also local in origin. The pedlars themselves are well-known folk types, very similar to the Foma and Erema mentioned in the discussion of "A Song for Erema." They are good souls, and they repent their petty deceits when trading with the villagers, but they follow the fate of the characters in the familiar folk tales in meeting a stupid death. They seem at times to be scoffers who have trouble with their fellow sufferers and peasants, although they themselves, of course, are of peasant stock. The tendency to drive a hard bargain and to stand apart is especially true of Tikhon, whose superstition also helps lead them into ruin. The portrait of the two main figures of the poem is therefore not a simple one: positive traits and negative ones are mingled. Nekrasov was intent on giving a plausible, realistic picture without idealization. He was also to a certain degree following the pattern of the folk tales about Foma and Erema, which also are usually cheerful at the beginning but end badly with the two characters as dupes. But in the main Nekrasov emphasized the pedlars' goodness more than their simplicity, and was thus able to achieve a tragic climax to their story.

Each section of the poem starts with an epigraph drawn from folklore, suggesting the contents of the coming section and setting the tone. Two of the mottoes are inventions of Nekrasov, namely the third and fifth, but they have the genuine ring of a folk saying. The poet could coin his own proverbs, or re-use and restate known ones very freely. He was able to do this without arousing the suspicion of invention, so that it is difficult for anyone but a folklore expert to identify his coinages. But sometimes his invented proverbs were actually hidden allusions. This may well be the case in the motto to the third section, which calls upon the peasant to "drink to the bottom." This is in fact an inversion of the sense of several similar proverbs of folk origin which refer to drinking. The purpose of the variation becomes clear only by means of a cross-reference to the poem "To Turgenev"; from the comparison with this poem the sense becomes that of enduring sufferings to the end for the sake of freedom.[10] This is a cryptic subtlety, and most certainly a refinement intended not just for intellectuals but for those who were also close readers of Nekrasov's poems. Such literary presuppositions must have been well beyond the range of understanding of peasants. Evidently the poet wrote on several levels at once; for his wide and disparate audience he supplied different possibilities in poems like "The Pedlars."

V *"Red-nosed Frost"*

Prince Kropotkin, in general not a great admirer of Nekrasov, considers "Red-nosed Frost" (1863) his "best poem." Many of Nekrasov's admirers and detractors both would agree with this opinion. It is one of his richest and most varied in style and content. It is one of his great works, a masterpiece, and justly famous. Parts of it always appear in school texts for Russian children, and it is a great favorite in anthologies of Russian verse. It is the despair of translators. In technique there are many similarities with "The Pedlars" and other, earlier poems about peasants; the adaptation of folklore themes and the use of popular speech in modified form, proverbs, lamentations and other folklore material are very much like that of the earlier poems. But in "Red-nosed Frost" the larger scope permits new combinations of song, description, and narrative. The greater length of the poem provides room for a panoramic view of peasant life and customs. Thus for example the fate of a peasant woman, briefly sketched in the figure of Katia in "The Pedlars," is portrayed here in detail. Katia is, to be sure, a precursor of Dar'ia, the heroine of "Red-nosed Frost," but she is a young girl whose full story is never told. Dar'ia is a wife and mother whose whole life and way of living is depicted in intimate detail. Nekrasov brought to bear his profound knowledge of peasant life, even to details of popular superstitions. His knowledge of folk customs was too intimate and accurate for the Slavophils, who heartily disliked the poem when it was first published in 1864. Almost all the folk sayings and phrases which Nekrasov uses in the poem have been recast, rephrased, and adapted. This was, of course, partly a formal necessity, since there are in folk songs no three-foot amphibrachs and no alternate-line rhyme scheme, the metrical pattern of the early sections of the poem.

But even in their altered form there are recognizable folk beliefs, folk medicine, and such superstitions as the rabbit crossing the road on Dar'ia's trip to the monastery, the falling star, and the raven on the cross at the monastery. In "The Pedlars" too the poet had shown the peasants' strange mixture of religious belief and old, pagan superstition, what is called their *dvoyever'e* or "double-faith." Nekrasov knew peasant psychology so well that he was able to make the transitions from religiously based customs to old, pre-Christian folkways without obvious stress. In reproducing the language of the peasants he keeps well in mind not only their mere speech habits, but also their psychology and the ways in which it expresses itself. Classic in this respect, and equaled only by the grief of mother Orina, is the description of the parents together after Prokl's death (II, 176): food, clothing, and indirectly suggested sorrow, all the more moving for the understatement, are all narrated in a few lines with great power and concision, the practical concerns and the formalities (expected by the mourning neighbors) being the framework by means of which the family's grief is expressed.

Syntactical influences of popular speech are evident throughout most of the poem; they affect word order, producing parallelisms, tautological verb constructions, repetitions, and also affect the forms of words, since diminutives of nouns and frequentative forms of verbs occur more often than they do in the literary language. Redundancies such as "Stado u lesa u tëmnogo brodit," or "Chërnaya tucha, gustaya-gustaya," and parallel constructions introduced by the negative particle are features of his stylization of diction in the direction of the folk song. The title itself is from a folk tale about "Morozko," the frost. But the actual narrative depends very little on any single source. Even the picture of the personified Frost, the great *voevoda,* is contained in no folk tale in such vivid and fully contoured form. To be sure his main attributes are those of the folk tales, especially his great urge to destroy, but the total picture is Nekrasov's own. The poet used fairy-tale motifs sparingly in his verse. The fantastic and make-believe do not figure largely in most of his poems, which are tuned more to realistic descriptions. Only by entering totally into the mind and heart of Dar'ia is the poet able to portray the projection of her fantasy from within and thus give her dream-figures their form and substance.

The structure of the poem is simple in its broad outlines, but subtly composed in its details. There are two main parts after the dedication to the poet's sister, the first entitled "The Death of a Peasant" and describing the events immediately following his death; the second entitled "Red-nosed Frost," the main section, recalling earlier, happier days, the illness of Prokl, the attempts to cure him, then Dar'ia's arrival in the forest and her death in the arms of the Frost. In the first part the author speaks and describes what he has learned of the death of Prokl and his funeral; he is the author-observer. The second part consists of the thoughts and feelings of the widowed Dar'ia. The actual sequence of events is narrated out of strict chronological position in order to shift the focus of attention to the dramatic elements. Thus the opening—the little horse in the drifts, the coffin, the dead Prokl, and his orphaned family—belongs chronologically after chapters six and seven. Chapters three and four are a digression on the fate of Russian women, opening with the famous lines:

> Three hard forms of fate fortune gave;
> The first: to marry a slave,
> The second: to mother a slave's son,
> The third: for life to obey the slave,
> And all these grim forms of fate
> Lay heavy on the women of our state.

Chapter five is a bridge passage, returning to Dar'ia. Chapters six through nine proceed in sequence and cover the details of the burial rituals, the digging of the grave, and a traditional lamentation for the dead Prokl, about whom we learn in other than general mourning terms only when the funeral procession is underway. Chapter nine portrays the grief of the neighbors and of the parents of Prokl. Chapter ten is a digression, harking back to the opening and the little horse that draws the coffin. Chapter twelve tells of how Prokl fell sick and how various folk remedies were tried without success. Here the reader's sympathies are indirectly invoked, for he feels the emotional stress and at the same time sees the peasants in the grip of ignorance and superstition. Not until chapter fourteen is the actual interment described. Chapters fifteen to eighteen retell, now in the interior monologue of Dar'ia, the trip to the monastery and the failure to save Prokl's life by religion-magic. From chapter sixteen on we hear the voice of Dar'ia, or with imperceptible transition we experience with her and share her thoughts and feelings, including the projections of her imagination. Recounted are her attempts to save Prokl's life, the days of past happiness and shared love, her worries about the future of her orphaned children, and gradually the transition is made to her own trip to the forest to gather wood, her numbness and weariness, her euphoria in the last memories of happiness, and her final succumbing in death to the embrace of Red-nosed Frost.

There are many rhythmic variations in the course of the poem; songlike cadences alternate with more emphatic stresses, so that the basic meter, the three-foot amphibrachs are modulated from section to section of the poem, or even replaced by other measures. The rhyme scheme changes too; monotony is avoided in this regard also. Some parts have run-over lines with pauses in the middle of the line, giving the impression of conversational speech tones. The length of the metrical line varies also, especially in Dar'ia's dream, and in some chapters four-foot lines alternate regularly with three-foot ones. Dar'ia speaks in dactyls in her famous monologue, so that together with the rhymed couplets a very different effect is achieved from that of other sections.[11]

All this wealth of forms and refinements in rhythm, rhyme, and sound effects did not come into being suddenly or at one time. The poet worked on the poem for many months, changing and adding. The first fragments of the final version were published in Dostoyevsky's magazine *Time* in early 1863. The sections printed were entitled "The Death of Prokl," and this is also the first title of the finished work. In the first version there was an ending according to which Dar'ia returned to her home and her children. The second version changed the main theme from the death of Prokl to the life and death of Dar'ia, emphasizing her positive traits and, together with the much increased role of Red-nosed Frost, made the poem quite different in subject. In its final form the poem centers on Dar'ia and her life and emotions, the theme of Prokl being subordinated to Dar'ia's experiences. It is interesting to speculate on the degree to which the political conditions of the time are reflected in the changes Nekrasov made from the first to the final version. He chose to emphasize more strongly the inner strength and resilience of the peasants in a time of doubt and government repression. The radical societies were driven underground or broken up by a government which was determined to suppress the peasant revolts at all costs. The failure of the Polish rebellion (January, 1863) meant also the end of any hopes for a large-scale peasant uprising in Russia too. *The Contemporary,* forced to close down for several months in 1862, was involved in polemic struggle with the liberals, whose writings reported again and again that the *narod* was not mature enough for freedom and not ready for representative forms of government. Under such conditions Nekrasov's sympathetic and moving descriptions of peasant life, of the peasant's love for work ("All their salvation is in work" [II, 170] writes the poet; even after his death the amount of work performed by Prokl is mentioned again), the loyalty and love of which peasants too were capable, were a political act of great significance. This was well understood by most of his contemporaries, for whom no overt political references were necessary. During the 1860's there were several publications by the Slavophils tending to glorify the simple rustic joys of the villages in idyllic tones. Some writers, like N. V. Uspensky, wrote tales of village life with an eye to the humorous effects they could achieve. In contrast with such trivial writing the stature of Nekrasov's achievement assumes its true significance. He captures the beauty and the many-sided truth of peasant life in "Red-nosed Frost" without condescension, without sentimentality, without creating an idyll, and in a richly varied artistic form.

VI *Satiric Poems*

Satiric thrusts, even if dispersed and effective only through their suggestiveness, are present in both "The Pedlars" and "Red-nosed Frost." "The Pedlars" has some traditional skepticism about the clergy and the czar, and Dar'ia's unsuccessful trip to the monastery can easily be interpreted as anticlerical. But the two poems are satiric only in passing and only by the implications of certain passages. During the decade from the publication of *Verses* until

1866, Nekrasov, however, also wrote some of his best satiric poems. During the late 1850's he planned several satiric poems which he did not complete until later; "On the Weather," for example, was started in 1858, and the first half completed in that year. Not until 1865 was the second half written. In the 1860's Nekrasov turned his attention to satire to such a degree that in 1865 it became the dominant type of poetic production altogether, and in this year alone he wrote no less than sixteen satires. Several large cycles of satiric poems were planned, but never finished, although individual poems from them were completed and published. Nekrasov was often thought of by his contemporaries, especially those who were conservatives or Slavophils, as being primarily a satirist. It was as a satirist that he was known to the censors and to the government; it was as a satirist that he was known to other journalists who entered into polemics with his magazine. On the staff of *The Contemporary* and later on that of *Notes of the Fatherland* was the greatest satirist of nineteenth-century Russia, Saltykov-Shchedrin, a friend and collaborator of Nekrasov's, so that guilt by association was operative here too. Soviet critics are uniformly enthusiastic about Nekrasov's satiric poetry and can hardly find words to praise it highly enough. But for a reader not emotionally involved with the targets of the satire or the reasons for them, the satiric poems are not so rewarding as the poet's other genres. The versification is often more glib and jingly than really poetic; the not always subtle ironic stance of the poet can become tiresome when sustained.

There are several reasons for the poet's turn to satire in the 1860's. Under Valuyev the government, with the reforms mentioned in Chapter 2, wished to give the impression of having become liberal and lenient. In fact this was merely a maneuver by Valuyev, and the government in practice retained all its old repressive measures. The exposure of this hypocrisy was one of Nekrasov's chief goals in his satiric poems. Satire, as we can deduce from his poems, should attack general and widespread evils, not narrow or personal targets, and it should expose the causes of the evils which it attacks. Such an approach is in line with the poet's general tendency to typify and seek the representative in all of his poetry. It is also, of course, consonant with his understanding of the methods of social criticism which he had shared with Belinsky in the

1840's. In this regard Nekrasov was consistent throughout his career. From his earliest critical reviews to his last satiric poems his fundamental attitude never changed.

In the late 1850's Nekrasov planned a large cycle of satiric poems that would deal with all aspects of contemporary Russian society. While the cycle itself, intended to be encyclopedic in its scope, was never finished, parts of it appeared in print: "On the Weather" (1858, 1865), "The Reading Room," "Recent Times," and "Ballet" are the poems which were published from the unfinished project. Two short comedies belong in this same category, namely "How to Kill an Evening" and "The Bear Hunt." Although not part of the original cycle, the satiric poems "Songs of the Free Word" (addressed to the "New Laws regulating the press" of 1865), and "The Court" (1867) belong in style and spirit to the poems mentioned above. Both the last two are a reaction to the hypocrisy of the new laws on censorship and control of the press, and both contain biting satire and irony both subtle and obvious. At the same time, especially in "The Court," the poet finds room for attacks on the timidity of the liberals, whose abject cowardice in the face of official disfavor was obviously comical to Nekrasov, who had had to live so long with a hostile government. The series of poems that make up "On the Weather" have some sections dealing with the lower depths of St. Petersburg, especially the first half. After twenty years Nekrasov returned to the theme of the down and out in the capital, eloquent evidence for the constancy of the poet's real concerns. The second, later part is based on the principle of the satiric contrast, especially between the rich and the poor, those who succeeded and those who failed, the sated and the hungry. "Ballet" is a report on the contemporary theater; but the author's impressions of the theater are only the starting point for a sharp attack on the capital's ruling caste and the high society which imitated it. The poem starts out with a vocabulary drawn from journalese and common prose conversation, but then turns to a rustic vocabulary. It is one of the curious examples not only of change of style within the same poem but also of his use of prose vocabulary and turns of speech. In "The Reading Room" Nekrasov satirized both landowners and members of upper-class clubs. Nekrasov himself often played cards at the exclusive English Club and knew very well the types which frequented it. As a rare deviation from his general principle of not naming individuals in his satire, the poet mentions several names in this poem: Count Tolstoy, Fet, Katkov, and Turgenev, although it is not they specifically who are being held up to scorn. In the middle of the satire the poet has placed a few lines defending his own position, and these lines are often quoted:

> Yes! but still the refrain of our songs
> Is sorrowful yet, we must admit.
> To change it we seem not to be able,
> Abide by it then we've decided.
> Be reconciled then with my muse!
> I know no other refrain.
> Whoever lives without sorrow and anger
> Loves not his native land.

VII *"The Railroad"*

The first railroad built in Russia was constructed from St. Petersburg to Tsarskoye Selo in 1837. The so-called Nicholas Road (St. Petersburg to Moscow) was opened in 1851. Nekrasov was never interested in technological developments as such, but he was vitally concerned for the human price paid for progress. The poet knew details of the construction of the railroad (1846–51) in part through a cousin of I. I. Panayev who was an engineer under the general supervision of Count Kleinmikhel'. The poem "The Railroad" (1864) is a topical poem in the best sense of the word. In it a contemporary problem is treated, after research and study, producing a poem with a factual basis addressed to a current condition. On the surface the setting is historical (it refers back at least thirteen years in time), but the basis of the poem is to be found in the contemporary confrontation of the exploiters with the exploited—a timely topic for the period following the peasant reform and the ensuing government reaction. It was written in 1863–64, but when first published it was dated 1855 in a futile attempt to lead the censors off the trail. But the censors understood the message immediately and issued *The Contemporary* a warning. This was no surprise to Nekrasov. When the manuscript was first submitted to the board of censors for inclusion in the impending fourth edition of the collected poems, they refused to allow its publication. In spite of this the poet decided to print it in *The Contemporary,* knowing in advance that he was taking a great risk. The preliminary warning the magazine received for printing the poem was the second one; according to the statutes a third warning would mean the suspension of *The Contemporary.*

The brief, ironic epigraph may be quoted in full: Vania: "Papa, who built this railroad?" Papa: "Count Pëtr Andreyevich Kleinmikhel', my son." The poem itself is in four parts: a picture of autumnal nature as observed by the author from the train's windows. Its serene beauty serves as a contrast with man's sad state. There follows a chilling description of the hunger and bad economic conditions prevailing in Russia. Hunger is called "the merciless Czar" who rules the world. The author's story of the true builders of the railroad refutes the poem's ironic epigraph. The third and fourth parts pose and answer the question as to who is to blame for the miseries of the workers who built the railroad, and by implication are responsible for the misery of the nation as a whole. The third section consists of the reply of the general to the assertions of the author. He ends by requesting the author to tell Vania the bright side of the story. The fourth section continues and completes the author's narrative, which is very ironic as he pretends to agree with the general and see things in a cheerful light. This is again a familiar form for a Nekrasov poem: a travel poem with a dialogue motif; and again the author is an observer, commentator, and sympathizer. The figure of the general is intended as typical of a half-educated reactionary who sees only the product and its profit, not the human suffering which went into its construction. In the second part, the author's account, there is a scene of great imaginative intensity as the author conjures up the shades of the dead who died while building the railroad. At this point he is suddenly no longer a narrator-observer but a participant who identifies himself with the dead workers and can say: "*We* strained under heat and under cold." In an unpublished variant to the late poem "To the Poet" Nekrasov wrote: "Two camps exist, as before in God's world: In one the slaves, the masters in the other" (II, 605).

"The Railroad" has as its theme the wide range of victims of oppression and the equally wide range of oppressors. Those who took advantage of the laborers were not just high officials like Count Kleinmikhel', but a whole series of greedy officials, down to corrupt petty police officers and the suppliers of food for the workers. These last get their due in the satire of the fourth section. The suggested range of oppressors may go even further: it has been inferred by some that the name of Kleinmikhel' is an Aesopian reference to the czar. The theme of the peasants' ability to perform hard work is familiar to us from "Red-nosed Frost," which describes the hard work demanded of peasants who till the soil, and the substance of the poem is the heat, sweat, and grinding labor of a peasant woman in the fields. In "The Railroad" it is a question of excessive demands made on the workers, and there is no question of joy in the performance of work, since they were laboring not in their own fields but for contractors who cared nothing for the human cost. But the poem is not just attuned to accusations, for it has optimistic notes too, although they are as much a hopeful vision of the future as an assessment of present realities:

Fear not for the fatherland beloved . . .
The Russian *narod* enough has endured,
Endured also this road of iron—
Will endure whatever God sends!
Will endure all—and a broad, bright path
With its breast it will pave,
This only is sad, neither you nor I
Shall live in this beautiful time.

In the different divisions of the poem the diction changes rapidly, although the poem has a unity in its basic tonality. Its four-foot dactyls and its steady, pulsing rhythm lend it a songlike quality even in narrative and explication. At times the poet achieves rich melody with soothing vowel harmony. An example of his favorite vowel *u* appearing under the accent:

Vse khorosho pod siyaniem lunnym,
*Vsiudu rodimuyu Rus' uznay*u . . .
*Bystro lech*u *ia po rel'sam chugunnym,*
*Dumayu dumu svoy*u.

"Dumat' dumu" belongs to popular speech rather than to high style. It is a phrase very common in Nekrasov, who obviously liked the sound of it; it might well be translated with a corresponding tautology in English: to think one's thoughts. Equally frequent is the phrase with the diminutive: "dumat' dumushku"; in the poem "Granddad" appear the lines:

Slushal—imeyushchii ushi,
Dumushku dumal svoyu (III, 16)

The language throughout is that of the literary standard, without peasant turns of speech. It is even rather formal, although it also avoids bookish vocabulary too and maintains its cantabile quality except for some conversational phrases near the end. The poem is only two hundred lines long, but within this limit the poet has achieved so much that the impression given is that of an epic.

VIII *Confessional Poems*

The effect created by the constant presence of a person speaking to the reader from the poem has already been noted as one of the characteristic features of a Nekrasov poem. There are so many poems in which the voice of the author sets the scene, guides the dialogue, and frames the story that at first glance it might seem that most of his poems are autobiographical in nature. But it soon becomes easy for the reader to distinguish those poems where the poet speaks in the first person in order to indicate his involvement and let his judgment be heard from those where the first person singular specifically denotes the poet Nekrasov. Thus the "I" of "The Railroad" is only within the given fictional limits to be identified with N. A. Nekrasov, while the person speaking to us in the next two poems we shall consider, "On the Volga" (1860) and "Knight for an Hour" (1862), is the poet himself. We have already had frequent occasion to remark that the poet may make personal digressions in poems whose main theme is not autobiographical, and that those which take as their starting point a personal confession soon may turn to broader subjects. The successful interweaving of the socially directed and the privately conditioned sets Nekrasov apart from most of his contemporaries.[12]

"On the Volga" and "Knight for an Hour" were originally planned as part of a larger, mainly autobiographical poem (perhaps cycle of poems) with the title "Knight for an Hour." Only the first and fourth parts were completed. The fourth part now has the title once intended for the whole cycle. The word "knight" in this context refers to his role as champion of the cause of revolution and reform; only for an hour could he feel that he, as poet and propagandist, had really contributed to the cause or accomplished anything worthy of his convictions. Both poems contain self-doubts, self-reproach, and uncertainty with regard to both his poetic gifts and his role in life. Both are poems of homecoming, of recall of his youth, and both are numbered among his most characteristic poems of penitence. In a variant to "Knight for an Hour," written in the album of a friend and not contained in the published version, his sense of failure is expressed even more strongly and bitterly. This variant is now published in Volume II of the *Complete Works,* pages 552–53. In part it reads:

> And the toiling, penniless people
> Pass before me with stern reproach,
> And in their face I read a threat,
> And in my heart suppress a tear.

The feelings of guilt from the alleged reproach of the *narod,* whose suffering he neither shares nor ameliorates, is wholly in the imagination of the poet. Far from threatening him, their literate leaders looked upon him as their own, as their very special hymnist.

The initial motif in both poems is given by the impressions of the author upon returning home. The autumnal features of the natural setting are exquisitely portrayed in intimate detail. Loving care and close observation are devoted both to the grand sweep of the landscape and to the little things that are dear to the poet. Even the flight of a bird evokes an exclamation of wonder and joy. But man and his condition, even more than the feelings of the poet himself, are never far from his mind. "On the Volga" recalls the poet's youth on the banks of the river, but it soon turns to the hard lot of the Volga boatmen, whose monotonous mournful cries are first recalled as the poet heard them, only half-comprehending, in his childhood, but then as he hears them again, understanding. The fourth section, which is a return to present time, refers to the new meeting of the adult poet with the *burlaki.* They have not changed, for they are still suffering and submissive. This provides the rhetorical question: "How much worse would be your lot in life,/ If you should cease your passive enduring?" This is the real climax of the poem, which has now moved from the autobiographical to the sociological.

In "Knight for an Hour" the opening is again a splendid evocation of the Russian countryside, and again the starting point is the return to the native fields. This time the poet's own feelings of guilt and insufficiency blend into a portrait of the poet's mother, and it is a picture of her suffering, her goodness and nobility that assumes the central place in the poem. With its fine descriptions of nature and the monument he set to his mother, this poem of Nekrasov's was a favorite with many of his contemporaries. The anapaestic meter is kept flexible in its different rhythmic effects and is readily adapted as the poet shifts rapidly from one scene to the next. The vowel harmony of the poem is one in which *o* and *u* predominate and alternate:

> *Ia stoyu potikhon'ku, bez shumu,*
> *Na pokrytom stogami lugu*
> *I nevol'nuyu dumayu dumu.* (II, 94)
>
> *Ia kruchinu moyu mnogoletniuyu*
> *Na rodimuyu grud' izol'iu.*
> *Ia tebe moyu pesniu posledniuyu*
> *Moyu gor'kuyu pesniu spoyu.* (II, 95)

There is a dramatic quality in both poems which stems in part from the frequent personifications, and creates the illusion of the poet amid animate, participant objects. At times the flow of narrative-description is interrupted by terse, aphoristic phrases, but without the didactic quality that usually distinguishes such statements in his poetry. "Knight for an Hour" closes on the reproach that he was fated to have bursts of creative endeavor, but never to complete anything. This may be taken only as self-recrimination, or it may be understood as representative of the lot of many intellectuals during the 1850's. The poem was conceived shortly after the break with Turgenev and at a time when many who thought as Nekrasov did became active revolutionaries, joined underground societies, and often paid the penalty for their illegal work.

Nekrasov did not go to prison or into exile. For this he felt guilty; but he was by no means alone, for many who were sympathetic to the cause of liberating the *narod* made their contribution, like Nekrasov, with their writing. Nekrasov contributed much more than just moral support to the revolutionary cause. Many of the underground activists were also contributors to his magazine in the 1860's, and were supported and subsidized by *The Contemporary*, one of their few legal forums. The periodical was the rallying ground for many of the radical intellectuals, a fact which was not unknown to the government. Nekrasov performed his greatest service, however, with his poems, for he enriched the poetry of his time with works of art which may still be read with enjoyment.

Not every poem combining personal feelings with other elements is as successful as the ones we have just discussed. Nekrasov loved Dobroliubov like a younger brother. But when he memorialized him in "To the Memory of Dobroliubov" (1864) his intense feelings and at the same time his desire to proclaim Dobroliubov's place in literature produced a poem whose solemn high style (it is written in iambic pentameter; iambs are the measure Nekrasov always chose for poems of pathos) tends in places toward the grandiloquent. The imagery is conventional too, and does not have the immediately visualizable quality so characteristic of so many Nekrasov poems. The line: "And his prophetic pen fell from his hands" could have been written by any versifier. The genuinely Nekrasov tones are heard in those poems in which personal feelings are expressed against the background of the *narod* and Russia's natural beauty.

The period from the publication of *Verses* until the final closing of *The Contemporary* in 1866 is a decade of rapid growth in Nekrasov's creative abilities and in the scope of his poetry. Most striking is the growing use of folklore in his verses. The pictures of rural life which he created during these years belong to the best in Russian literature. The village harvest or the funeral in "Red-nosed Frost," which also contains the imaginative and beautiful picture of the winter woods, the autumn landscape of the Iaroslavl' region and the river Volga, and the awakening of spring in "The Green Sound" are unforgettable impressions of the Russian landscape. But most appealing are the portraits of people, especially peasants. Here the poet's sympathies are awakened, the pictures are drawn with love and admiration, and the figures of the pedlars, who are drawn sympathetically even in the critically realistic details, the peasant children at play, the old woman's memories of her youth without regret, the dignified and muted sorrow of mother Orina for the ruined life of her son, Dar'ia's profound love and loyalty for Prokl and her measureless grief expressed with sure and suggestive restraint—these are significant and enduring creations.

CHAPTER 5

The Years of Fulfillment

O muse! our song is sung,
Come close the poet's eyes
In death's eternal sleep
O sister of *narod*—and mine! (II, 405)

AFTER Nekrasov read his humble poem of loyal obeisance to Murav'ëv, the hangman of Poland, in the English Club, his friends were dismayed and dumbfounded and his enemies delighted. Nekrasov's despair was deepened not only by the failure of his efforts to save *The Contemporary,* but by his own sense of guilt for having betrayed his principles. His actions at this juncture have always been a stumbling block for his biographers. Nevertheless some things may be noted in explanation, if not in extenuation. The purpose of his reading poems expressing his loyalty to the regime is clear: he wished to save *The Contemporary,* not just for himself, but as a forum for his colleagues and their ideas. It is also apparent that the step must have cost a great effort of will. Regrets and self-torment were not long in coming. They find their expressions in poems like "The Enemy Rejoices," written under the immediate impressions of those difficult days. The first poem of the year 1867 is addressed to some unknown friend who sent to Nekrasov a poem entitled "It Cannot Be," an anonymous poem repeating the accusations of hypocrisy and betrayal, but with the refrain: "it cannot be." Nekrasov was very touched by this expression of faith in him in spite of appearances, and he dedicated to this unknown loyal supporter the poem "I Shall Soon Die." The opening words (the title) might well serve as a motto for this section of our book, for the remaining years of the poet's life were spent in the shadow of impending death, with many moments of depression and melancholy. There are many poems concerned with the state of his health, with his general dejection and his sense of the shortness and sadness of life.

"I Shall Soon Die" has an elegiac tone that is new in Nekrasov; there are, to be sure, similarities with earlier poems, such as "Be Silent, Muse," written in the same mood of a sense of failure and approaching death, but the sustained minor key, the retrospective view of a longer span of life, and the more intensely felt guilt for a specific act set it apart from anything written before. Loneliness, a common theme since the early 1860's, the loss of friends, and the consciousness of having betrayed the cause make this one of his most gloomy poems. At moments of self-appraisal like this, the poet invariably recalls his youth again with bitterness, half as lament, half as explanation and excuse. "Under fateful oppression I spent my childhood/ And my youth—in tortured strife." But the refrain and the final message of the poem is his request for forgiveness: "For the drop of blood, shared with the *narod,*/ Forgive my sins, o mother country, forgive!"

The 1870's were years of constant personal reassessement for Nekrasov. Loneliness and increasing preoccupation with his slowly worsening health combined with moments of doubt in his mission in life to create moods of profound melancholy. The tendency to look back over the span of his life became stronger with the passing years. This retrospective frame of mind finds one of its reflections in his poetry in the return to elegies and other traditional forms of poetry. The "Three Elegies" of 1873 mark a renewed interest in the Russian poetic tradition. The first elegy has slight echoes of Pushkin in its iambic tetrameter and in its diction. The second is an elegiac romance with all the traditional requisites: roses, azure skies, and nightingales. The conventional language and formal structure are reminiscent of the poetry of the first half of the century. The third elegy has echoes of the diction of Lermontov, especially in the last quatrain. Most of the poems which we have discussed up to now have been innovations, have opened up new vistas in Russian poetry, and mark departures in form and style. He was to continue this trend in poems like "Russian Women" and "Who Can Be Happy in Russia?", but at the same time he seemed increasingly to feel the need for seeking rapport with the great classical tradition founded by Pushkin and Lermontov. The two tendencies always existed side by side in Nekrasov, who came more and more to express personal feelings in classical forms and to use his adaptations of folk forms for less intimate verses.

Among his personal poems of the 1870's is the poem with the suggestive title "Despondency" (1874). It opens with the words: "You have burned down, nest of my fathers!" But this exclamation is uttered without sentimental regret, for this is a poem of homecoming with a difference: the poet accepts the fact of the loss of his ancestral home with calm, even with joy. The spirit of the place remains, with its conflicting memories, and the poet, happy to be out hunting again, has at first no mournful emotional ties with the place connected in his mind with the tyranny of his father. As we shall see later, home seems very different when the poet is remembering his mother. But the poem is not so much about a return home as about the poet's spirit of dejection and his feeling of failure:

> My heart is sick, my sorrow grows,
> *Narod! Narod!* No heroism in your service
> Was granted me, bad citizen that I am,
> But passionate, sacred concern for your fate
> I bore till the grave. (II, 369)

In the poem he speaks of himself as a soldier of the cause, a wounded veteran who asks to be judged not by his enemies, but by those who are "reader-citizens," the word "citizen" having again that specially charged meaning which it had in the opening poem of *Verses.* There are didactic aphorisms in the poem, some quite often quoted. Unusual are the frequent direct appeals to the reader, who is really constantly addressed. The words "alas" and "fateful," becoming now more and more common in his verse, occur here as part of the coloration of the poem. But there are still passages which give evidence of the undiminished musicality of Nekrasov's verse:

> . . . *a vol'ny veter niv*
> *Smetayet sor, naveyanny stolitsei* . . . (II, 364)

With the repetition of the vowels *o, e,* and *i* placed among consonants which show the repetition and alternation of *n* and *v,* together with liquids and sibilants, the suggestiveness of the sound underlines the motif of the wind.

In the next year, 1874, "Elegy" renews the themes of the preceding poem. The word "service" is the key word of this formal poem, written in strict iambic hexameter. Of his own service he says that his lyre was always dedicated to his *narod.* And often quoted is the line: "The *narod* has been freed, but is it happy?" This question—and so many of his poems end in questions—is one of his best-known commentaries on the emancipation of the serfs. Later, in "How They Fête a Coward," he wrote: "In the life of the peasant, now free,/There is poverty, ignorance and darkness." Again the word "alas," rare in his earlier verse, appears in emphatic position. In rhythm and style the poem echoes Pushkin's "The Village." Nekrasov prized the poem very highly as one of his most successful in several years.[1] "To a Poet," dedicated to the memory of Schiller, is also one of the poems among the poet's own favorites. He worked hard and long on the poem, refining, rephrasing, and striving for the utmost concision. The language is reminiscent of that of Pushkin and Lermontov; the vocabulary is that of classic solemnity. The many imperatives create a tone both oratorical and imploring. Phrases like "magic torch," "priest of art," and "age of blood and the sword" belong to the high rhetoric of the early nineteenth century. Since it is a poem of high style and pathos, it is written in iambic pentameter. Belinsky had been enthusiastic about Schiller, whom he prized as the great poet of freedom. Chernyshevsky wavered in his opinion of Schiller, sometimes valuing him as a poet who was an eloquent champion of freedom, at other times having doubts both about his rhetorical style and the inconsistency between his poetics and his style of living. Nekrasov was constant in his high estimation of Schiller.

I *The Role of the Poet*

The role of the poet, always important in Nekrasov's thinking, became one of the dominant themes of his reflective poetry in the 1870's. It is the calling of the poet to show man the path to the good and the truth. It is the duty of the artist to lead man to love and brotherhood through beauty, beauty here understood as the service of the truth. Schiller would have agreed with this definition of the high calling of the poet, but of course the poem is less a portrait of Schiller than a statement of Nekrasov's own beliefs and an expression of his hopes.

The last few years of Nekrasov's life bring poems to his wife Zina, to his muse in many moods, and ever again poems about his health and his sense of approaching death. In a poem to Zina (II, 404) he again looks back upon his life as one that was not fulfilled, and finds a formula for his failure that is half regret and half explanation: "The struggle prevented my being a poet,/And songs kept me from being a fighter." This tone of self-deprecation was not the only note he struck in his personal poems, for he sometimes felt a surge of pride in having at least remained true to his ideals. The long, unfinished poem "Mother" was meant to be a monument to the woman who was not only his mother, but also an ideal and a symbol of woman's suffering and nobility. In the fragments which are published, the memory of his mother quite naturally leads to personal confession. Well known are the lines: "This muse was given me by fate:/She sings at her free will,/Or is silent, like a proud slave." (Cf. his letter to Tolstoy, X, 331–32.) The second chapter opens by recalling that the poet left home while still a youth "to seek fame in the capital city." At twenty, he continues, he returned home, too late to find his mother still alive, and the next lines recall, in soft, flowing language, the scenes of garden and house once made dear to him by his mother's presence. There is no bitterness here, as in the very different memories of home in which the figure of his father is dominant. All sights and sounds serve now only to remind him of his mother, now lost to him through death, but still present through that spiritual force which was her nature. The third chapter is in the form of a letter from the poet's grandmother (here considered for fictional purposes to be Polish) to his mother, expressing her fears for her daughter in the faraway depths of Russia. The letter becomes fragmentary, and gradually the thread of the narrative is lost. But a noble beginning was made, and the early part of the poem contains some of the poet's sweetest, softest language. He was bitterly unhappy that he was unable to complete the poem in a fashion worthy of the person it was meant to honor.

In view of the form in which "Mother" was left, the poem does not present as full a picture of his mother as that in "On the Volga" or "Knight for an Hour." In these latter poems, however, the figure of his mother is given in generalizing terms, stressing her nobility of character and her tolerant patience rather than portraying individualizing traits. The poet left behind no poem in which his mother is painted in individual, specific colors, for she was, in memory, always a symbolic figure for Nekrasov. With time she seemed to blend imperceptibly with other heroines of the poet's imagination.

Among the poems of Nekrasov's last years, those dedicated to Russian children hold a place of honor. The town pedlar, the bees, a bear as the supposed driver of a troika—these are some of the themes in the first cycle dedicated to Russian children in 1867. "General Bruin," the bear apparently driving the troika, is a special favorite that has inspired several artists to illustrate it. In 1870 the poet again published two poems for Russian children, "Grandad Mazai and the Rabbits," and "The Nightingales." The first of these tells how Grandad Mazai rescues rabbits from a flood by catching them and taking them to safety in his boat. It is simply a tale of a peasant's love for all things living. The second, however, although it has a similar theme, namely the peasants' love for the song of the nightingales and how they were protected from snares and nets, also adds a note of social criticism. At the end a child asks its mother if there is any place on earth where people can find a refuge like the one for the birds, a place where they cannot be reached by taxes or recruiting for the army. No, answers the mother, but if there were such a place, the peasant women would immediately take their children there. Even in a poem for children the poet could not repress his urge to comment on the social conditions in Russia. The symbolism of the snares and nets once used to catch the nightingales was obvious enough even for the censors.

During the 1870's Nekrasov continued to write poems about the *narod* and its fate in the forms he had developed in earlier years. "Another Troika" is a good example of a "travel poem," a form familiar to us from the earliest poems, used to set the scene for a vignette of contemporary life. The opening lines echo those of Pushkin's "The Wagon of Life," but only as a reminder and without any intention of parody. The author observes a troika driving along with a prisoner under guard; under the circumstances of the year 1867 no commentary is necessary to allow one to guess that it is a political prisoner on his way to exile. The poem consists of a series of rhetorical questions addressed by the author to the prisoner, expecting no answer of course, and speculating on the possible reasons that such a young man might be a prisoner on his way to Siberia. The refrain, slightly varied in each strophe, is that no answer is given and the wagon continues on its way. Only in passing, as one of several possibilities, is the suggestion made that the youth might have wished "to destroy the government." But in the days after Karakozov's assassination attempt on the czar, the sight of troikas with prisoners under guard was so common that everyone, including the censors, could easily interpret the poem.

Equally clear is the message of the poem "The Mother" (1868), not addressed to the poet's mother, but about the mother (or wife) of a political exile. The mother's form of address to her children: "Unfortunate ones!" betrays the sense of the poem, since "unfortunate," as we have already pointed out, was the usual term for an exile. At the end of the short poem the author advises the mother not to weep for the future of her children, because:

> There are times, there are whole centuries,
> In which there is no more beautiful wish
> Than that to wear a crown of thorns. (II, 317)

II *Satiric Poems*

Those poems in which Nekrasov's revolutionary sympathies found an indirect expression are usually more striking, more effective, and more esthetically satisfying than those in which he resorted to overt satire. The last two poems discussed have a concrete setting, a picture of people, and a message that is unobtrusive but unmistakable. The power of suggestion, framed by a background of description and narrative, works freely and effectively. But Nekrasov could not resist the urge to write straight satire. He loved the open, direct attack, the reduction to the absurd, and the opportunity for caricature. He was remarkably consistent in his methods throughout his whole career as a writer. "A Fellow of the Forties" (1867) represents no advance beyond the techniques which the poet had already developed in the 1840's when collaborating with Belinsky. The poem is even somewhat reminiscent of "A Moral Fellow," and like that poem it is a short, caricaturing, ironic confession told in the first person. Like all Nekrasov's poems of this category it lacks subtlety, and it suffers from the same limitations imposed by the first-person form that "A Moral Fellow" does. The date of the title is not to be taken too seriously. It is rather clearly aimed at the poet's contemporaries of the late 1860's. No more subtle in its attacks on the bad effects of early, aggressive capitalism is the poem "Recent Times" (1870). It is in the form of a mock address, portraying the English Club under Nicholas I and the early reign of Alexander II. The occasion for the poem was the one hundredth anniversary of the club in 1870, and the poem has therefore a historical basis. But the biting satire and the heavyhanded irony make it one of the poet's less appealing poems, although for fanciers of the genre it is a fine specimen of *feuilletonistic* satire.

The most ambitious satire Nekrasov ever carried out is the long "Contemporaries," 1875. Part of the poem goes back into the 1860's, when some early drafts were made. Nekrasov did a great deal of research for the poem, combing newspapers, books, memoirs, and other sources for material for the poem. It is a portrait gallery, a kind of rogues' gallery in which successive types, considered by Nekrasov to be exploiters and enemies of the people, are skewered on his satiric pike. There are two main divisions: in the first the observations of the author take place in the individual rooms of a modish restaurant, and in the second in the big common hall. The long series of individual portraits is aimed chiefly at the coalition of the aristocracy by birth with the new moneyed classes. High officials are among those included as parasites and enemies of the *narod.* The formal aspects of the poem vary from section to section, the poet using vaudeville couplets, popular songs, and constantly varied items from magazines and other sources. The poem even has its dramatic moments: the self-abuse and recriminations of Zatsepin, who weeps at the song of the Volga boatmen. Under the stress of sorrow for the loss of his son and in response to the mournful song he recants and repents his ways; but only for a few moments, since his repentance is not genuine, but quite fleeting and hypocritical. At this point the height of the poem is reached in an ironical unmasking of hypocrisy. Zatsepin's sorrow is soon cured by playing cards, all is as before, and on this wry note the poem ends. The author's voice has an important place in the poem, especially in the first part. The reminder of the condition of the *narod,* the song of the Volga boatmen, is the climax of the poem before it trails off in the antics of Zatsepin.

"Contemporaries" is a very long poem with many variant readings, representing the results of months of work and effort. The motive for undertaking such an ambitious project must be reconstructed from what little external evidence we possess. Apparently Nekrasov wished to capture in his verse the many types of people who were living at the expense of others. He had already, in "The Sorrow of Old Naum" (1874), dealt with the *kulak,* the rich peasant who takes advantage of his poorer fellow peasants and loves only money. The urge to portray the upper classes, both the aristocracy and the new plutocracy which emulated it, and to satirize them in all their many manifestations, must have been very strong. The poem dedicated to his mother remained a fragment, and several other projects were set aside in order to complete the broad canvas of "Contemporaries." Even "Who Can Be Happy in Russia" was neglected for the sake of satire directed at the ruling cliques, although this poem too is full of satiric thrusts in the same direction.

The chief target of "Contemporaries," regardless of the particular type being portrayed at any moment, is the all-pervasive hypocrisy of the upper classes. Most offensive to Nekrasov is insincere or simulated sympathy for those less fortunate financially. This is a theme which runs throughout the poem. The "hero" of the first part, the fat Prince Ivan, is an old clown, and is not taken seriously. Therefore his accusations of his peers and his criticism of them are to be understood as Nekrasov's own views only in a qualified sense. His chief function is to prepare the way for Zatsepin's grossly hypocritical tears and ostentatious repentance. The main purpose of the poem, the one thread which runs consistently through the mass of details, is to unmask hypocrisy in all its many forms in a direct, frontal attack. With its documentary basis and the fact that many persons can be identified with living models, the poem might have become a kind of human comedy of the 1870's. But the realistic elements are overpowered by the grotesque qualities of the poem. If Nekrasov had been content with less caricature and less obvious irony, he might have created a historical document of the first rank.

III *Decembrist Poems*

Fortunately not all the poet's creative energy was absorbed by satire. Although he did much preparatory study for "Contemporaries," he did even more research for his poems on the Decembrists. Over thirty years after the Decembrist revolt of 14 December, 1825, the decree of amnesty for the survivors of the exile in Siberia was signed on 26 August, 1856. Only nineteen of the original group were alive and able to return in 1856. For the most part they were warmly greeted by the populations of both Moscow and St. Petersburg, for an aura of heroism still clung to them. In the minds of many it had been the best and noblest of the Russian aristocracy which had participated in the revolt. Prince S. G. Volkonsky, who served as one of the principal models for Nekrasov's portrait of a Decembrist in "Grandad" (1870), was received with special honor and affection. Volkonsky supplied many traits for Nekrasov's hero, among them his fondness for gardening and for manual labor of many sorts. But in important respects the model and the hero of the poem differ. Volkonsky returned from Siberia chastened and reconciled to the error of his ways; Nekrasov emphasizes the unaltered devotion of his hero to his early idealism and his continued interest in politics and the new realities which he found upon his return. In a letter to the son, M. S. Volkonsky, Nekrasov, still preoccupied with the Decembrist theme, wrote that he wished no essential errors or inaccuracies in his poetic reporting on the fate of Volkonsky.[2] But in drawing the typified, composite figure of the grandfather, he used only those facts and those character traits which were appropriate to his purposes. Nekrasov was writing only of the unrepentant Decembrists, not of those who gave up, recanted, or sought to regain imperial favor. Since all the returning exiles were under police surveillance, it may be that several were perhaps more discreet than they might otherwise have been. Nekrasov did rely heavily on sources from the Decembrists themselves; one of the chief sources for the factual basis of this poem as well as for "Russian Women" is the memoirs of Baron A. E. Rozen, to whom Nekrasov owes his description of the settlement of free peasants in Tarbagatai, now a town in Mongolia.

Nekrasov had developed the technique of comparing the conditions of prereform Russia with those after the emancipation of the serfs in such works as "The Bear Hunt." He continued, after "Grandad," in the satire "Recent Times," and in a different style but with the same purpose, in "Russian Women." The poet was able to depict prereform Russian conditions in such a way that the analogies with the contemporary scene were clear to his readers. In his idealizing description of Tarbagatai, more a Utopian settlement of the poet's imagination than a real village in what was then Siberia, he was able to show the prosperity and happiness of peasants who had been granted "freedom and land"—*Zemlia i volia* was the name of a secret revolutionary society to which Chernyshevsky belonged before his exile. Such allusions were not lost on contemporary readers. But the poet was not interested only in topical allusions. The Decembrists were valuable to him not only as masks through which he could speak of contemporary conditions but also as the first great Russian revolutionaries. Their cause, in his historical understanding of it, appealed to him. He saw in the Decembrist revolt the first great move against autocracy, carried out by the leading spirits of the time, the flower of the Russian aristocracy. He was interested also in one of the reasons for their failure, namely their neglect of popular support. The task was too great for a handful of conspirators, who failed to mobilize even the soldiers under their direct command, and the revolt lacked the broad base of popular support which it needed for success. For all the idealizing that takes place in his poems about the Decembrists, there is also a detached, clear insight into their weaknesses and their errors as well as sympathy for their highminded idealism. Along with their faults he also saw and appreciated the historic significance of the first modern attempt at revolution in Russia.

Although Nekrasov's letters of this period refer to his having read and studied much about the Decembrists, biographers sometimes tend to make a mystery out of the poet's turn to historical subject matter during the late 1860's and early 1870's. The matter probably needs no explanation; it is in any case unfair to the poet to expect nothing but contemporary topics in his poetry. Perhaps the expectation that if he should choose historical material he would then write about some peasant or Cossack leader such as Pugachëv or Sten'ka Razin is behind the assumed need to explicate what is really not so astonishing. The subject was popular; many interpretative as well as artistic opportunities were given by the theme; and after all it was treated in verse by other poets too, for example, Mikhailov and Ogarëv. For all the radical intelligentsia the Decembrist revolt was and remained the great historical deed of the century. It would be strange indeed if Nekrasov did not seize the opportunity to place the event in what he considered the proper historical light. And at a time of general stagnation in political development it was a chance to hold out hope for the future. The fictional time of the poem is 1856, that is, before the emancipation of the serfs, so that Nekrasov can prophesy the future freedom of the serfs; but his view of the future goes far beyond this, for by implication, especially in the Tarbagatai section, the distant future is envisaged in hopeful colors.

One of the basic messages of the unreconstructed returning grandfather is that social injustices must be combated and never compromised with. For his listening grandson he enumerates wrongs that he had observed in his youth and prophesies their removal in the better future. He is above all a teacher, who devotes his energy to instructing the young Sasha and encouraging him to become a fighter for the right. After the bleak and terrible descriptions of the lot of the peasantry in the 1820's, the conditions of 1856 mark some slight improvement, but still the serfs were not free. The pictures of earlier and contemporary life make all the more striking the grandfather's optimistic faith in the future. Thus the poem comes to be at the same time an historical poem, a topical, contemporary poem, and a vision of the future.

In form the poem consists mostly of a dialogue between the old Decembrist and his grandson Sasha. The old general is drawn with sympathy and admiration; his personality and undiminished powers, and the strength and conviction of his spirit make him one of the grand figures in Nekrasov's verse. Sasha, on the other hand, remains rather pale by comparison; he is a type, an object of the grandfather's teaching, but of course he is also the hope of the future. The opening is planned to cast an aura of mystery over the missing grandfather, who has not yet returned from exile.

Sasha's curiosity is aroused, but never satisfied with adequate answers to his questions. The constant refrain, also repeated later by the old Decembrist, is: "When you grow up, you'll find out." The grandfather, who does not actually appear until the fourth strophe, is never called a Decembrist, nor are there any references to the revolt itself. Even his exile is not termed exile, but a stay in a far distant place, and the reasons for the stay are never made explicit. The grandfather is introduced as an imposing cavalier of the old school, with his courage and enthusiasm unbroken. He is pictured as being at peace with his fate, which he affirms, and his eagerness and spirit are youthful as he teaches his grandson, embraces private soldiers, chats with peasants, or tills the soil.

The author's language used in describing Grandad is often very high style, full of Church Slavonic forms, but the old general's own speech has many elements of the popular, spoken language. "Freedom and work for man will produce wonderful wonders," or "The sight of the people's distress is unbearable, my friend; happiness consists in seeing contentment round about," and other aphoristic sayings come from his lips freely, lending a slightly didactic tone to his language in spite of the colloquial forms. But when his speech, now hardly directly addressed to a child anymore, reaches heights of intensity, then the poet no longer fills his language with diminutives or the post-positions "-ko" or "-to," but turns to a higher lexical level and such rhetorical devices as questions, exclamations, thoughtful or dramatic pauses; and again and again he emphasizes that no feeling, intelligent person, having seen and experienced what Grandad did in his youth, could fail to act: "Who then, in whom honor is still awake,/ Who would assent to this?" These lines form a refrain like the promise addressed to Sasha. And the poem ends on the promise that the grandfather will at last tell his grandson the story of the Decembrists and explain everything. But within the poem itself all has already been explained to the reader.

IV *"Russian Women"*

"Grandad" is only the first of Nekrasov's poems about the Decembrists. The portrait of a Decembrist returning unrepentant from exile was only the beginning. The revolt itself, and the glorious role that women played in its aftermath, still remained to be told. From the beginning to the end of his career Nekrasov was attracted to the fate of political exiles and prisoners; among his poems about them are: "Before the Rain," 1846; "The Unfortunates," 1856; "Thanks to Lord God," 1863; "Another Troika," 1867; "The Mother," 1868; and by implication and prophecy also the final part of "Who Can be Happy in Russia?" The role of women in society, at a less heroic level, of course, than the princesses who were wives of Decembrists, occupied many pages of the *Notes of the Fatherland* during the late 1860's and 1870's. Articles on women's rights appeared frequently in its pages. In literature too novels and stories had already begun to take the emancipated woman seriously. Chernyshevsky's novel *What is to be Done?* is one of the earliest. Turgenev's novel *On the Eve* has an emancipated woman as heroine. It should be remembered, however, that the heroines of Nekrasov's "Russian Women" belong to the 1820's; interesting also is the fact that neither Princess Trubetskaya nor Princess Volkonskaya took any part in the actual revolt or in the revolutionary activities of their husbands.[3] But their trip to Siberia in voluntary exile in order to join their husbands was a political act of the highest order. Czar Nicholas was perfectly aware of this, a fact which is evident from his attempts to have them stopped by the governor at Irkutsk.

This political factor in the story of the two princesses appealed to Nekrasov, who saw an opportunity to present a view of the Decembrist revolt from a new perspective. But of course he was interested in more than merely giving new interpretations to historical data; he was fascinated by the people involved, for themselves and not just for their symbolic or historical value. This is clear not only from the warmth and sympathy with which they are portrayed, but also from the fact that Sasha from the poem of that name and Dar'ia of "Red-nosed Frost" live again in the aristocratic ladies of "Russian Women." He describes the princesses with the same words as those used for Sasha and Dar'ia: blonde curls, tall stature, firm gait, and pretty face. These are patently conventional and standing epithets to a large degree, and lead us back to folk poetry and its ornamental, undifferentiated epithets. The form of description is deliberate, however, since Nekrasov is able thereby to suggest the typical Russianness of the princesses and artfully imply their common heritage with the peasant women to whom he had set a monument in the earlier poems. The impression of solidarity with the common people is strengthened by the actions of the princesses as well as by the responses of sympathy and support of the *narod.* On the other hand, the poet stressed the coldness of the officials with whom the ladies came in contact.

Individual characterization is achieved by emphasizing a certain trait and singling it out for special use. Just as in "Grandad" the old general's loquacity and urge to instruct form a dominant personality trait, so is, for example, the determination of Princess Trubetskaya a distinguishing feature. In addition to the scenes of dialogue in direct confrontation, a further dramatic quality is lent to the poem by the fact that Nekrasov allows the women to reveal their character in word and deed. The variant readings of the poem illustrate eloquently the efforts the poet made in order to characterize by direct speech and action rather than to describe or narrate from the author's perspective.

The poem is written with many purposes in mind. It is not merely the struggle with an autocratic regime that Nekrasov wishes to portray, but the relationship of the revolutionaries to the *narod.* In stressing the positive and close nature of both sides of this relationship, the poet is to a degree idealizing and drawing a picture somewhat colored by wishful thinking. But in the documents and memoirs which Nekrasov studied so carefully there is also evidence of the warmth of the relationship, and expressions of sympathy for the fate of the revolutionaries occur in the poet's source material, a fact which attracted him from the first. A third aspect of the material with which he was working also finds expression in the poem, namely, the rights of the women to their own lives. The right to decide the course of one's own life and dedicate it to a cause is a major theme of the poems about the two princesses. For this reason the poet devotes so much space to Princess Volkonskaya's struggle with her family. Her moral courage is shown in her conflict with her father, who is also a man of great will and determination. Her reasons for joining her husband in Siberia, like those of Princess Trubetskaya, are at first personal and reflect her profound love for her husband, for whom she is willing to sacrifice everything. Only gradually does the poet unobtrusively suggest the political implications of the women's decisions; only gradually do both become aware of the ideological import of their actions and grow to be sharers in the ideals and idealism of their husbands. Through this new awareness they are able to bear the hardships of exile, buoyed up not only by unselfish love but by the profound conviction of the rightness of the cause. The heroines' gradual moral growth is shown in harmony with the popular sympathy for their fate.

The first of the two poems which make up "Russian Women," "Princess Trubetskaya," has two major divisions. In the first her departure, her farewell to her father, and her difficult trip are narrated in such a way that flashbacks serve as punctuation and contrastive elements. Her happy, sheltered youth is recalled, with the contrasting picture of bitter scenes of Russian life in the 1820's for the common people. The flashbacks are woven into her trip with great artistry. The poet achieves impressive effects with great economy of language. Upon her return from a honeymoon in Italy, the princess is struck by the harsh conditions of life in Russia and asks her husband if all the land is so dismal and if there is not a trace of happiness anywhere. "You are in the realm of beggars and slaves!/ Brief was the answer." But this shock at the sorrows of Russian daily life after the idyllic honeymoon in Italy, the gradual growth of the princess' mind and character commences. Sleeplessness and oppressive thoughts disturb her. Later, her condition as an exile makes her a sharer of the people's sorrow and leads her to closer bonds with the *narod.* She gives money generously to exiles as one of her gestures of sympathy. The contrast between her protected childhood and the grimness of contemporary reality is Nekrasov's way of narrating without commentary but still making sure his message is clear.

After the above comes the description of the uprising itself, impressive and dramatic in its concision. The main source is again the memoirs of Baron Rozen, as well as the official, published documents. But Nekrasov compressed the description, eliminating many details and concentrating on the suggestive high points. This dramatic scene is followed by the visit with her husband in prison. The premonition of the hardships that await her are woven into the narrative, and in general the princess' dreams and memories are blended with her observation of the actuality surrounding her in such a way that they reinforce each other. In all there are eight dreams of the princess that are interspersed among the descriptions of the landscape and of the princess' condition in her waking state, so that both contrast and continuity are maintained.

The second division of the poem is a dramatic dialogue with the governor of Irkutsk, who had imperial orders to detain her and if possible to prevent her continuing her journey. In the opposition of official will and the princess' determination Nekrasov provides himself a splendid opportunity to depict the princess as an ardent patriot. Three times the governor tries to persuade her to give up her journey. After each attempt he makes her wait for days in order that his warnings may take effect. But in the conflict of wills with the governor the princess wins a wonderful moral victory, and the poem ends with the half-expressed sympathy of the governor, won over by her nobility. Most politically significant is the scene in which the governor offers to let her continue if she will sign away all her rights and privileges as princess and become a commoner. With casual indifference, amounting even to disdain at the trifle, the princess signs and in the same breath renews her request for horses to continue her travel. Some of her replies to the governor's arguments are ringing words that are often quoted, e.g., "Contempt for our hangmen,/ Consciousness of right/ Will be our true support." When first published in *Notes of the Fatherland* Nekrasov added an annotation in which he declared that he had decided not to touch on the political implications of the story of Princess Trubetskaya. Such a note was intended for the censors and the credulous.

Baron A. E. Rozen, in his *Notes of a Decembrist*, published in 1870, emphasizes the importance of the interview of the princess with the governor. He also reports the readiness with which the princess signed away her class privileges. The scene as vividly portrayed now in the poem, however, is Nekrasov's development of the source material and is in style, tone, and emphasis his own invention. The figure of the governor is gently ironized, but it is not totally negative, since he is shown as a faithful servant carrying out orders. Only at the end does a personal touch become evident when a tear falls as he bids the princess farewell. In the interview itself he is a worthy opponent, capable of subtle psychological moves in his attempts to dissuade the princess, but also capable of sympathy and humanity. His final defeat honors him as a person.

He is seen through his actions and his words alone, but in describing the heroine Nekrasov does not shy away from Romantic language, appropriate enough in speaking of the 1820's, but also the right language for the Romantically minded princess. Siberia as seen through the eyes of the heroine is a romantic wilderness, for all its hardships. Quite different and much more concrete and realistic are the descriptions in the voice of the author.

Nekrasov received permission to read her as yet unpublished memoirs from the son of Princess Volkonskaya, M. S. Volkonsky. He adapted the memoirs very freely, although he was careful not to change essential facts. In addition, he used other memoirs, records, documents, and conversations with survivors and their friends and relatives. Only when he had completed a great amount of research was a beginning made on the poems comprising "Russian Women." The fact that the poem had a carefully documented basis had interesting and varying consequences. We have already quoted Mirsky's opinion that it was too close to the original. Dostoyevsky, in his *Diary of a Writer,* took issue with the poem because it was too free and not factual or realistic enough.[4] There were also details to which he objected, among others the lines which refer to falling off a ridge in Siberia, and to the scene of reunion in the mine where the Princess Volkonskaya kisses her husband's fetters before kissing him. This, he believed, was psychologically false and an undesirable embellishment. As a matter of fact this little detail is contained in the princess' memoirs and is taken over directly by Nekrasov, who invented nothing here.

The structure of "Princess Volkonskaya" is similar to that of the earlier companion poem. It is in the form of the memories of the princess as told years later to her grandchildren, so that again the direct speech of the heroine takes precedence over the author's voice. The first three chapters deal with the events preceding her trip to Siberia, the last three with the journey itself, ending with her reunion with her husband in the silver mine. The first chapter gives a brief biography of her father, General Rayevsky, continues with her marriage, her married life, and her husband's burning of his private papers. In the second, her child is introduced as an emotional tie that might bind her to her home. This is followed by her hasty departure for St. Petersburg and the story of her efforts to obtain news of her husband, then by her decision to follow her husband in spite of her father's opposition. The third chapter continues the struggle with her family, a counterpart in its test of wills with the scene between the governor and Princess Trubetskaya. It is in this scene that her moral courage and her profound love for her husband are shown in word and deed. The fourth chapter, although apparently a digression from the course of the narrative, serves the purpose of demonstrating the great amount of support and the number of approving allies that the princess has for her decision to follow her husband.

One of her chief supporters, who encourages her and helps to confirm her convictions, is the poet Pushkin. There is a historical basis for the friendship of Pushkin with the Volkonsky family, although Nekrasov has taken some liberties and has invented some things here. Pushkin was also sympathetic to the Decembrist cause. Nekrasov wished to emphasize this fact, but he also went further and gave considerable space in the poem to the Pushkin section. Above all else he stressed Pushkin's support for the princess' decision on moral and ideological grounds. There is, however, another important part of his farewell speech to her that shows that he envies her the fact that she will be leaving behind the world of high society and its false demands. She will be giving up class pretensions and entering a world where character alone will determine her fate. In ascribing these views to Pushkin, already accepted by the nation as its great classic poet, Nekrasov had several purposes in mind. One of the principal ones was to show his contempt for class privilege and the life of the aristocracy. For this reason this scene with the poet, told as a warm memory of the princess', is an analogue to the scene in which Princess Trubetskaya signs the paper renouncing her class rights.

The fifth chapter resumes the narrative and is concerned to a large degree with a description of the conditions of life in Russia at the time. The princess' own relation to the *narod* is emphasized by her stay with the woodcutters, who refuse pay for this kindness. The sympathy and support of common people in the humble church confirm the feeling of rapport between the princess and those of humble station. In the final scenes of the sixth chapter the same theme receives a variation when the commanding officer of the silver mine displays arrogance and hostility in contrast with the good will and kindness of the simple soldier. A community of suffering and sympathy is established between the exiled princess and all whom she meets who are not minions of the government. The sixth chapter brings the reunion of two people of great moral stature, the princess and her husband, among fellow exiles who are still unbowed by their lot and are unrepentant in spirit. It is a triumphant ending but also represents an idealization on the part of the poet, since there were those Decembrists who did repent and seek to ingratiate themselves with the czar.

The poet permitted himself such idealizations without destroying the essential factual basis of the poem. But he did not take material from his sources indiscriminately. Rather he achieved his effects of convincing realism by selecting carefully only those details which served the general purpose of the poem. In the early versions of the poem, now available to the reader in the variant readings of Volume III, the temptation to adopt interesting items from the memoirs may be seen at work. Details which make the prose memoirs vivid turned out to be entirely out of place in the poetic context Nekrasov created. One can watch the progressive elimination of matters which reveal the princess as charming and very feminine, but which detract from the heroic image which Nekrasov was establishing. The fact that the *kibitka* first chosen was not large enough for all the household comforts and servants accompanying the princess, was retained until the final version, but finally omitted as not being consonant with the total picture of a journey of hardship and sacrifice. The poet even tried to preserve the small clavichord which went along to Irkutsk, but eventually eliminated it, since it was clear that this detail would have been detrimental to the heroic stature and grandeur of the scene with the governor. The homely and intimate details of the memoirs have a very different quality in their total effect from the picture created by the poet. Historically it is interesting to know that even exile had its comforts in those days.

A careful study of the variant readings has led Chukovsky to the conclusion that Nekrasov was striving for a "monumental style." [5] Chukovsky overstresses the monumental style of the poem, which is not constantly striving for grandeur and heroic effects, but soars over a wide range of tones, and rises to the high rhetoric of pathos only where it is appropriate. However, he is right in showing how the familiar details of everyday life, present in large number in the early drafts, were either eliminated altogether or were made much more concise. That which trivialized, in spite of the appeal of the homely detail, was discarded in favor of typifying and representative elements. And the poet also substituted his own inventions for the facts of the memoirs. One example of this is the change at the very end of Princess Volkonskaya's journey. According to her account the reunion with her husband took place in a building of the prison. Nekrasov moved the scene to the depths of the mine, gaining greatly thereby in poetic possibilities.

"Russian Women" is the finest epic work that Nekrasov created. It has remained a favorite with the reading public since it was first printed. As a monument to the splendid heroines of the Decembrist revolt it has no peers in Russian literature. The poet wrote this masterpiece at the height of his powers. The language achieves a wide range of effects, dramatic, descriptive, evocative, with brilliantly concise narration of historical events. Yet critics, notably other poets and writers, have often been reserved in their judgments. The reason for this is difficult to discover, for close reading reveals excellence in nearly every line. There are dreams revealed in interior monologue, great flights of fancy, wonderful vignettes of the Russians and the Russian scene in the early and middle century, and all this is artistically interwoven with a narrative that gains in momentum from the contrastive flashbacks which serve to highlight it. And above all the emotions of the heroines are communicated with convincing intensity. The poem remains as fresh and rewarding today as when first published. As a work of art, combining epic, lyric, and dramatic qualities, it is unsurpassed among Nekrasov's poems.

V *"Who Can Be Happy in Russia?"*

During the time of its composition, however, the poet had already started an even larger project. The long epic poem "Who Can Be Happy in Russia?" occupied the poet's attention from 1863, when it was first planned, until his death fourteen years later. Work on the poem was not continuous, but it never ceased to claim his efforts when other projects were completed. It is a poem about the friends, enemies, and members of the *narod*. In many ways it is the sum and synthesis of Nekrasov's creative works, a compendium of his views and attitudes and the forms in which he chose to express them. It is also compendious and panoramic in its scope, to the detriment of artistic unity, which is lacking in this long poem of loose structure. The first part, including the prologue, was finished in 1865; the second part was not completed until 1872, since work on the poem was interrupted by the composition of "Russian Women." The third part, "The Peasant Woman," was finished in 1873. The fourth part received the form which has come down to us in 1876, although the poem as a whole was never completed. Both the first two parts are separate and self-contained units. The third part is also only loosely related to the poem as a whole. The central, unifying idea of the more or less independent parts is the demonstration that conditions in the country after the reforms were still bad, but that the energies and inherent strength of the common people were not destroyed. The fourth section also is intended to show that the self-awareness of the peasants was growing rapidly, and that some of the intelligentsia had now taken up their cause.

These brief statements of the intent of the poem sound didactic and stodgy, which is unfair to a poem that is bright and sprightly, full of songs and musicality, and has a full range of tones. The motif that sets the poem in motion is that of travel. Seven peasants from seven different areas meet on a highway and decide to wander together until they can find the answer to the question of who can live happily and freely in Russia. They come from villages with allegorical names such as "hard-battered," "destitute," "harvestless," or "hungry." The use of such names of villages in poetry is an old device. In Russian literary poetry Nekrasov's immediate precursor in this respect is Krylov. The initial notion is a promising one, for it grants the poet a large measure of narrative freedom as the peasants travel through the Russian lands, interrogating people and debating their problem. In the Prologue the fairy-tale motif of the magic tablecloth is introduced. The tablecloth serves them food and drink whenever they are hungry, thus relieving them of work and allowing them to concentrate on their mission. This is told in a humorous tone, since the peasants' leaving their work and families for such a quest is naturally not to be taken too seriously. Before they have even started their journey they fall to fighting with one another; the poet is smiling both at the seriousness with which they take their problem and at their tendency to brawl. A gentle irony lies over most of the scenes in which the seven peasants figure prominently. But he also allows them to engage in rather subtle dialogue, since, with all the mild irony, he also wished to demonstrate the natural wit and shrewdness of the peasants. A good example of their native intelligence is evident in the scene with Obolt-Obolduyev, who speaks to them with hypocrisy and seeks to mask his real intent. The peasants pretend to go along with his statements, and they apparently answer quite simple-mindedly, but actually they are clever in their answers and only simulate failure to comprehend.

The original plan consisted of a series of encounters for the peasants which would bring them into contact with all classes and callings in Russia, from the lowest ex-serf to the czar himself. But this plan of complete coverage was given up during the course of the composition in order to concentrate on pictures of certain "positive heroes": Iakim Nagoi, the great worker; Ermil Girin, who ends in prison for his role in opposing a landowner; Savely, the hero of all Russia, who rose up against a German overseer and was imprisoned and exiled; Kudeyar, who kills the oppressor Glukhovsky, a landowner; Matrëna Timofeyevna, who is fierce in protecting herself and her son and whose story illustrates the continuing hard lot of peasant women. The word used for Savely is *bogatyr*, an old word for a legendary hero with echoes of the heroic age of the *bylini*. The last hero, Grigory Dobrosklonov, is in some respects an idealized reminiscence of Dobroliubov.

In the course of composition the plan of the poem underwent several changes, so that the beginning, with its fairy-tale atmosphere, is gradually lost from view. More and more Nekrasov ceased to rely on the travels of the seven peasants, with the result that at the end their fate is not settled nor their quest brought to a conclusion in the sense in which it was begun. The stories of the heroes just enumerated gradually replaced the motif of travel; the condition of the *narod* came to be illuminated from the biographies of individuals rather than from a series of interviews. The unity of the poem in its narrative structure is impaired by the abandonment of the original device, but there remain adequate compensations in the portraits of people. And in a way the question of who can live happily in Russia is never lost from sight. The village priest, the merchant, and the landowners all give some answer to the question. And they all answer in purely materialistic, selfish terms. The priest, for example, wants to find "rest, wealth, honor"; he seems most concerned about his low income and lack of comforts. Some former serf-owners cannot become reconciled to the new, post-emancipation conditions and try to preserve, in caricatured form, the old ways of life. Spirituality of any sort, idealism, or a concept of service to others the peasants fail to find in any of the privileged classes. No one will admit that he lives happily in Russia. On the other hand the so-called positive heroes mentioned all have in common deeds which were unselfish in motivation. The last hero, Dobrosklonov, has a vision of the future awakening of Russia which is famous and often quoted. He is the one who is happy, because he is a dedicated fighter for freedom who is sustained by his idealism in the face of certain exile and suffering.

To enumerate the folkloristic elements in the poem would be tantamount to retelling most of it. The *bylina* "How the Birds Live in Russia," from Rybnikov's collection of folk tales published in 1862, may have suggested the title, and several other parallels with tales from the collection have been identified by folklorists. But many songs and proverbs that seem to be drawn from an oral folk tradition are actually Nekrasov's own inventions. To this folkloristic basis Nekrasov added the basic, grandiose irony that it is seven peasants who will resolve the question of who is happy in Russia. They are the judges of the whole country, the arbiters who will decide the question, introduced at first half-playfully, but gradually assuming monumental proportions. From a humorous variation on a folk tale to the climax in the vision of Dobrosklonov, the poem grows in depth and breadth until it seems to span the fate of all Russia. Of all of Russia that is important, it should be noted, since Nekrasov does not deal with the government, the high officials, or the ruling classes, except for some isolated minor aristocrats who are satirized. What is important is the *narod;* its fate is seen as the determining factor for the future.

Present in the poem are idealization and grandeur of prophetic vision, but there is also much homely realism and good-natured irony. Not all peasants are heroes. The village elder, Gleb, is an example of a peasant who rejects his status as peasant and goes over to the side of the landowners. A more subtle scene is that in which the peasant Luka, pondering the priest's answer to their key question, also thinks in materialistic terms. The poet wishes to show that the task of enlightenment has barely begun. One can hardly demand of the peasants that they think in higher terms than those of the people supposedly their betters. Nekrasov maintains a humorous distance from his peasants, describing their excesses, especially in drinking, along with their positive virtues. But their vices are seen with tolerance and without anger, whereas their virtues, namely their strength, their ability to work hard, and their courage, are portrayed with fondness and admiration. There is also some humor in the portraits of the negative characters, who are usually characterized by stressing humorous details.

The last part of the poem no longer keeps to the perspective of the peasants but is told largely in the author's voice. At the same time the style changes to a more pathetic, high style, and the simple similies taken from popular speech give way to extended metaphors, except of course, in the many interpolated songs. The critic T. A. Besedina has counted one hundred lines of similes in the poem.[6] Twenty of these are made up of proverbs and riddles. The poet made such generous use of proverbs for the sake of their laconic brevity and compactness as well as to illustrate popular speech. Even so he often shortened them and made them more concise, although most proverbs are naturally aphoristic. When using folk riddles Nekrasov often turned them about and partially resolved them, taking up into the simile the implied answer to the riddle. Few proverbs were taken over directly, since he often changed the proverb to fit a different context, thereby giving the original saying a totally new meaning. Sometimes the proverb is kept intact but presented in such a different context that it comes to serve a very different function. In one case words traditionally spoken by the bride were assigned by Nekrasov to the mother.

Since brevity and compression of the original into fewer words is the chief method Nekrasov used in weaving proverbs and riddles into his verse, the end result may be only an allusive hint. This is a delight to folklorists, but it is quite possible for an innocent reader to be baffled. One obvious effect of such uses of folk similes and sayings is to give a popular, folksy tone to the poetry. Another is the impression of concision and condensation, although at times this kind of shorthand use of simile may result in exaggeration, as for example in the prologue to the section "A Peasant Woman," where Matrëna Timofeyevna is introduced as "a cow, not a woman." This is intended as a compliment, for the same verses describe her as peerless in her village, but the comparison is a dubious one. Of all the similes noted by Besedina, only a few are actually based on true folk proverbs; those that are original with Nekrasov sound so much like popular sayings that only an expert can distinguish them. The poet was original and creative in this field, and his ability to coin folk sayings with a genuine tone is equaled only by his skill in adapting or composing original folk songs.

Metrical variations are frequent throughout the poem. The basic form, modulated to give different rhythms and tonal effects, is that of iambic trimeter with two final unaccented syllables. The rhyme scheme shifts from section to section in order to avoid monotony in the short lines; there are frequent internal rhymes, some in the full lines, some also in the interspersed two-beat lines. Often the poet saves the grammatical object for the end of the sentence, or sometimes for different emphasis the verb appears in final position. The end of the line or strophe, as the place of highest emphasis, usually contains the key word of the sentence. For stress at the beginning of a line he often uses an exclamation. Caesura is more frequent in this poem than in Nekrasov's other poems; the caesura is not generally an important feature of his verse, which normally flows in even cadences, but whenever he wishes to make the rhythm of the poem more emphatic he interrupts the line with the caesura. The lexical level of the poem is deliberately kept low, since the poet's intention is to make poetry out of everyday language. Nekrasov always found delight in the common people's language, in its inventiveness, and in its turns of phrase. In addition to the many proverbs, riddles, and folk songs which Nekrasov employed, there are also his own aphoristic lines of social criticism:

> You work alone,
> When work is done,
> There stand the three you owe:
> Our God, the Czar, the master. (III, 94)

Similar lines are scattered through the poem, but without rendering it didactic in tone, since most are kept within the basic tonality of folk songs and speech. The poem contains a vast store of information on folk customs, rituals, and forms of rustic living. For this and for its portraits of folk-heroes it can still be read with pleasure. But it is, in spite of its wealth of forms and virtuosity in versification, not on an artistic level of achievement with "Red-nosed Frost" or "Russian Women." The Soviet critic Egolin calls it Nekrasov's "most powerful work," an opinion other Soviet critics would not dispute. Although it has passages of great power and beauty, its interest for the modern reader is more historical and folkloristic than esthetic.

CHAPTER 6

The Enduring Nekrasov

> His was a heart wounded in the very early days of his life, and it was the wound which never did heal that was the inception and source of his whole lifelong passionate and suffering poetry.—F. M. Dostoyevsky

NEKRASOV arrived on a Russian literary scene that was rich in great achievements. He became the heir of forms and styles developed, cultivated, and brought to a high degree of perfection before his own beginnings as a poet. By the time Nekrasov had written the first poems he considered worthy of inclusion in *Verses,* a noble tradition of poetry, from the intimate, confessional lyric to the epic breadth of *Eugene Onegin,* had been established in Russia. The canonization of Pushkin was completed during Nekrasov's first years in St. Petersburg, if indeed it had not already taken place during Pushkin's lifetime. The place of Lermontov in Russian letters was secure before Nekrasov started to edit *The Contemporary.* Gogol's position was more controversial, and he was less quickly admitted to the Russian pantheon by universal agreement. But his popular fame and his approval by important critics were an accomplished fact dating from the publication of the first volume of *Dead Souls* in 1842. Therefore Nekrasov was in some respects in the unhappy position of one born too late, and his situation may be compared to that of the dramatist wishing to compose tragedies in the shadow of Shakespeare, or the poet working on a version of *Faust* in the Germany of the 1830's.

In assigning a place in the history of Russian literature to Nekrasov, the biographer or critic is faced at once with a problem of relative evaluation. Historians of Russian literature traditionally speak of the middle of the century, the period of Nekrasov's great productivity, as an age of prose. Sir Bernard Pares, for example, writes: "Lermontov only left behind him one poet: the greatest of Russian folk-poets, Koltsov. There followed an epoch of prose. . . . The neglect of verse in Russia lasted right until the end of the 'seventies'. . . ." [1] This view, not original with Pares, has been repeated by some other writers in one form or another that it has become a canon of criticism. The notion that poetry did not revive until the 1870's and really flowered again only with the Symbolists toward the end of the century naturally affects the evaluation of Nekrasov's place in literary history, since he must be viewed in the shadow of the great novelists. It also raises the problem, less important for us, of placing in the proper niche a poet like Tiutchev, whom Pares, in the context quoted, calls "the greatest poet of his day." It is not our intent to question this traditional view, but it may be qualified and put in its proper perspective from several points of view. The first, and perhaps most obvious for readers of this book, is the immense popularity which Nekrasov enjoyed in the period from the 1850's until his death in fame and acclaim in 1877.

At his funeral the head of the procession was formed by two peasant women in traditional costume who carried a wreath with the inscription: "From the women of Russia." After several funeral orations had been delivered, F. M. Dostoyevsky stepped forward and spoke the words which head this chapter. He also voiced the opinion that "in our poetry Nekrasov was last in the line of those poets who appeared with their 'new word.'" [2] Dostoyevsky, who also held the view that Nekrasov did not really understand the Russian soul as well as he, Dostoyevsky, did, was able to see Nekrasov in perspective better than most of his contemporaries. He realized that Nekrasov had indeed been original and had come with a "new word." "For instance, in the past, there had been Tiutchev, a greater and more artistic poet, and yet he will never occupy so conspicuous and memorable a place in our literature as will unquestionably be assumed by Nekrasov. In this sense, among the poets [i.e., who appeared with a 'new word'] he must be placed right next to Pushkin and Lermontov." When Dostoyevsky stated this opinion in his speech, a voice in the crowd shouted that Nekrasov was *greater* than Pushkin and Lermontov, and several people repeated this cry. Our conviction lies with Dostoyevsky's brilliant prophecy and not with the unknown enthusiasts who uttered "greater." Pushkin and Lermontov occupy an unchallenged, unique position as the greatest poets of the Russian language. But it is interesting to hear the voice of the people, even when one cannot share their critical judgment. For many in the late 1870's the notion that Nekrasov was greater as a poet than Pushkin and Lermontov was natural and not at all astonishing. But it is also clear that many held him in such high esteem because of his ideology and not because of his art. The remark of Dostoyevsky's, namely that Tiutchev was greater as an artist, is not isolated, but a commonplace in literary history. Nekrasov, however, has always had the greater appeal for just the reasons given by Dostoyevsky.

Nekrasov's limited reputation beyond Russia's borders is owed in part to the enormous difficulties in translating him adequately. But it is also owed in large part to the dominance of the novel in the 1850's and 1860's, a remarkable period of the flowering of the novel in Russia. Turgenev, L. Tolstoy, Dostoyevsky, and Goncharov published masterpieces of world literature during these years. If one were to select the greatest and most famous contributions to world literature produced in Russia, most of them would fall in this period, and all would be in prose. Judged by these standards of fame and world-wide acceptance, there is nothing in verse in this epoch which can stand beside the works of the novelists listed above. Perhaps in this connection the career of Turgenev is representative. His early creative energies were devoted to poems and dramas, genres in which his achievement is of a high standard. But he turned to narrative prose, and his fame rests on his novels. In Russia, Nekrasov's "Sasha" is often mentioned together with Turgenev's *Rudin,* but beyond its borders there is no question of their relative fame.

We may concede then that Nekrasov lived and published in an era in which prose dominated the scene, and rejoice in the great epic works the age produced without making further comparative judgments. But there is another factor affecting the estimation of Nekrasov's place in letters, and that is Nekrasov's relation to his predecessors. Even in his own time Nekrasov's relation to Pushkin was controversial. For many of his contemporaries the poems of Nekrasov were a new departure, disturbing innovations which seemed to reject the classical heritage. Far from seeing in his poems the continuation of a great poetic tradition, writers like Botkin, Druzhinin, Annenkov, and usually also Turgenev, considered his verses to be prosy negations of the Pushkin-Lermontov standard. Among other things they objected to his vocabulary, which seemed to be drawn from journals, or from peasant speech and other nonliterary sources. The subjects on which he chose to write were also not in the grand tradition. His skill in versification, his control of metrical form, and his wealth of rhythmic modulations went unnoticed. The question of purity of genre troubled many; his poems are difficult to classify even today, although in retrospect it is hard to see how this could prevent appreciation of their melody and richly varied tone color. The disarming simplicity and directness with which Nekrasov spoke to his readers about humble events of daily life seemed to lack art and certainly lacked artfulness. The public was accustomed to confessional poetry of the most intimate kind from the classic poets, who had spoken directly to the reader about private, innermost feelings, but usually within stylized, conventional forms.

Nekrasov's verse also has a large confessional element. As we have frequently pointed out, however, it emerges from a different context and has a very different point of departure from the classic forms. In most of his characteristic poems there is a fictional character whose fate and feelings are presented, and one hears the voice of the author, who places the figure of the poem in a precisely located framework and who indirectly suggests the responses the reader should have. The reader is not alone with the hero of the poem, but feels the presence of a guide who is prompting the attitude the reader should take. If Nekrasov had been content to write about his love for an imaginary Chloë, or his philosophical reflections on the state of the cosmos, using Classical mythology as a ready form of symbolic reference, he would have been immediately understood and appreciated by the esthetes of his day. The only question remaining for an evaluation of his poetry would have been his success in filling correctly and mellifluously the metrical form chosen for the fictional invention or the abstract consideration.

During Nekrasov's lifetime much confusion arose over what seems to later generations an idle dispute over false alternatives.

But in the 1850's the quarrel over the legacy left the nation by Pushkin took the form of opposing, in the form of a false dilemma, Pushkin's sublime, ethereal, and exquisite verse to the worldly, pedestrian prose of Gogol. The Gogol school (the "natural school") sinned as much as the Pushkinites in accepting the terms of the alternative. As each party came to exaggerate and to define more exclusively its own position, the advocates of social criticism began to lose sight of esthetic criteria and to search only for accusatory and tendentious writing, while the apostles of pure poetry hardened their hearts against all poetry which was not concerned with eternal verities in rarefied form. Either extreme seems grotesque to a modern reader, and fortunately the debate was only theoretical and hardly affected actual poetic practice, but we must remember that the controversy was taken quite seriously in its day. To praise either Pushkin's verse or Gogol's prose at the expense of the other may seem ridiculous now, but the writers of the mid-century used these names as battle cries for their cause. The political cleavage coincided with the poetical, since the "pure poets" were either liberal or conservative, and the natural school was radical. Nekrasov personally kept aloof from the extremist positions of both sides and quietly combined in his writing the heritage of both Pushkin and Gogol. His successful combination and continuation of this dual legacy is one of his great contributions to Russian literature.

I *Nekrasov's Relation to Pushkin*

The very first poems which Nekrasov wrote, even before he went to St. Petersburg at the age of seventeen, bear the unmistakable imprint of Pushkin. Nekrasov knew Pushkin's verses well at a very early age, absorbed them, memorized them, and never ceased to bear deep within him their sound and cadence. All through his life there recur the moments when the Pushkin style re-emerges in his poetry; whenever he writes poems of great pathos and seriousness, he fills again the Pushkin forms with his own feelings. Nekrasov made constant use of Pushkin. He quoted him in his letters, in his prose, in his verse, often quite freely, sometimes inadvertently altering the words quoted. Some of these free quotations are clearly made from memory. Sometimes whole lines occur; frequent use of Pushkin's locutions is a constant feature of Nekrasov's writing, private and public, throughout his life.

Pushkin remained for Nekrasov the great master, the supreme model and mentor, whose gift to the nation must be cherished. Again and again in his "Notes on Journals" he presented Pushkin as a model for the youth of the nation, and as a poet whom the nation should read and appreciate for his high ideals and sincere love of freedom and not just for the smoothness and brilliance of his verse.[3] When the poet Pushkin is portrayed in "Russian Women," it is again the pathos of freedom, the disdain for high society and its pretensions, and the contempt for autocracy which Nekrasov sees as his distinctive traits. It is quite possible that Nekrasov, with his wide connections with printers and publishers, knew some of Pushkin's poems in manuscript before they were published. No edition of Pushkin during Nekrasov's lifetime was free from the selective filter of censorship. Yet Nekrasov recognized in Pushkin the hero of freedom, the sympathizer with the Decembrists, and the social critic. He felt called to take up this heritage and continue it in his own fashion, as a successor not by imitation but by further development of tendencies he noted in Pushkin. The trends which he either knew or sensed in the great poet he continued, drawing his inspiration from the late poems and from the direction in which he believed Pushkin was developing in his last years. It is true, however, that when Nekrasov goes back to Pushkin forms, he very often turns to the Romantic odes and the high style of the early Pushkin.

The early works of Pushkin are usually referred to as Romantic. In some of his poems of the 1820's there is evidence of the influence of western European Romanticism, notably the poems of Byron. But if we take the Romanticism of western Europe as our standard, then there is hardly a real Romantic movement in Russia. Or we may state it another way, namely that the great classical period of Russian poetry happens to coincide with a degree of Romanticism. Without going into the complexities of the specific situation as it existed in Russia in the 1820's and 1830's, we may note that there were poets who dealt with the glorified national past, who wrote subjective love lyrics in the confessional style, who took as their subjects the fanciful, mythical, or the fairy tale, and other themes which we conventionally associate with Romanticism. None of the poets whose names have survived, however, really lost contact with the reality about them, and they never ceased to be concerned with the problems of the here and now. Therefore we may say without punning or unduly oversimplifying that Russian Romanticism, in the hands of the great poets, was basically realistic. Moral and social concern is evident in Pushkin and Lermontov, both of whom responded to the conditions around them. Their imitators, the lesser poets who have been justly forgotten, trivialized their inheritance from these masters in the 1830's and 1840's. Such poets were the targets of the satire of Nekrasov and the ruthless criticism of Belinsky in the 1840's. But in general the transition from a degree of Romanticism to what we call Realism is mostly a matter for Russian literary critics, who are able to discern individual differences and nuances which do not need to concern us. For the American reader there is a rather clear continuity, with some differences due to personal style, but in practice there is hardly a school or movement with clear contours, if we ignore the polemics and propaganda.

Nekrasov's profound respect and admiration for Pushkin needs no further commentary. We must not forget, however, that Nekrasov also found it easy to parody him. In 1846 he wrote "A Woman Like Many Others," in which he parodied not only the figure of Tat'iana from *Eugene Onegin*, but the style of the sections describing her. Most often, however, Pushkin-like forms are a sign of high seriousness rather than parody. "Poet and Citizen," for example, is intended to remind the reader of Pushkin. In the opening lines of "The Unfortunates," the "Bronze Horseman" of Pushkin is paraphrased; the echo of Pushkin's poems is meant both as a reminder and as a contrasting view of St. Petersburg. In "News" (I, 202) he echoes *Eugene Onegin*, chapter VI. The irony here is not directed at Pushkin, but at an empty life of distraction in which poetry is an idle embellishment. In "The Official" (I, 96) he echoes Pushkin's "To the Defamers of Russia." "Happy is the Gentle Poet" contains echoes of *Eugene Onegin*, as does also "Life's Holiday," whose title may also come from Pushkin's poem. Parodistic quotations, allusions, and reminiscences are frequent in the poems just cited. The use of Pushkin in his verse does not arise from lack of piety for the great poet, but it serves the purpose of poking fun at his imitators and those who tried to write in his style. Nekrasov took no credit for his own skill at versification;

thanks to the models of Pushkin and Lermontov, he said, anyone could write smooth verses. To do so, therefore, is no merit.[4]

Pushkin's Decembrist verse is in its pathos akin to Nekrasov's poems of freedom. Our poet commanded the "high" style of Pushkin whenever he wished to, so that it is misleading to speak of his alleged "lowering" of this style to the level of everyday prose. Not all of Pushkin's verse is drawn from sublime vocabulary; he made use of everyday words in his poems wherever he felt it appropriate. It is also not helpful to speak of Nekrasov's subject matter as tantamount to a rejection of Pushkin: he too had solved in his own way the question of the level of subject matter and style appropriate to poetry, and he had concluded that any theme or object was of indifferent value as the theme of poetry. But it is true that in Pushkin's early poems there were suggestions of an attitude of "art for art's sake," as for example in a poem like "The Rabble," 1828. To a degree Pushkin had a double view of life: an esthetic and a practical one. Nekrasov did not share this discrepancy between the life of the mind and life as a citizen in the same way; in theory at least he held the same ideals both as a poet and as a citizen, even though he often admitted that he had failed to achieve a happy synthesis. In retrospect it is remarkable that Nekrasov relied on friends and critics who had such tendentious and nonesthetic views of literature as Chernyshevsky and Dobroliubov. In view of their standards it is small wonder that the poet was often dissatisfied with himself, and that he could not consider his poetry a "deed" or a contribution to the cause—which according to Dobroliubov it could not be. It is not astonishing that he was often depressed and melancholy. His crisis of conscience is probably as much the result of this source of irritation as of any other cause.

During the 1850's the proponents of pure poetry made up most of the well-known contributors to *The Contemporary*. It was a period of close cooperation with them, most of whom were too important to be alienated in a time of trouble. Compromises were made in publishing their contributions, but not in the principles held by the inner group of the staff. The policy of the magazine remained what it had always been, and indeed it became more aggressive with the advent of first Chernyshevsky and then Dobroliubov. Turgenev, Druzhinin, and P. V. Annenkov naturally also made some compromises and showed considerable tolerance toward the radical critics who now surrounded Nekrasov. It was just at this time that Nekrasov's most important statements about Pushkin appeared; apparently the close collaboration with the liberals made the poet feel that the time had come to establish firmly his own views of the great classic poet. Contemporaneously Annenkov was busy with an edition of Pushkin, the most complete up to that point, but still heavily censored and without much material available to later scholars. In the articles during 1855–56 Nekrasov took a quite independent view of Pushkin, relying neither on Annenkov nor his opponents. He emphasized Pushkin's greatness, his sincerity, his desire to enlighten, his devotion to art —which is identical with the search for truth—and the manliness with which he bore his suffering and his oppression at the hands of the government. This praise was by no means at the expense of Gogol, nor set in contrast to him, since Nekrasov did not believe in such an opposition and intelligently allowed for many kinds of talent.

We mentioned earlier the profound influence of Gogol. Gogol was, next to Pushkin, the greatest and most lasting influence on his style and approach to subjects in both prose and verse. Nekrasov saw in him a humane satirist whose laughter pervades his satire and whose integrity relieves the bitterness of his observations. Just as Pushkin remained the great model in verse, so did Gogol remain his standard for all the great prose of the era. Thus he praised Turgenev, Tolstoy, or the plays of Ostrovsky by pointing out the resemblances to Gogol, and he used the degree of affinity with him as a criterion of excellence. For Nekrasov, Gogol was, in the broad sense of the word, a poet, since poetry in his view consisted in the vivid portrayal of the unembellished truth. Poetic truth may be harsh or happy, or grotesque as it often is in Gogol, but whoever can convey it convincingly and with sincerity is for Nekrasov a great writer.

II *The Influence of Lermontov*

Less complicated and in some ways less important is Nekrasov's relation to Lermontov. Lermontov is usually classified, at least for his early verses, as a Romantic. His beginnings were in subjective, very personal lyrics.[5] But he moved rapidly in his short career toward greater objectivity. His last poems have notes of protest, satirical views of autocracy and other features of Russia's backwardness; his main themes were national and regional, and he is one of the greatest poets of local color in Russian literature. These aspects of his poetry could not help but appeal to Nekrasov. Lermontov's prose too was appreciated by Nekrasov at a time when he was establishing his own style. *A Hero of Our Times,* and especially the unfinished tale *Princess Ligorskaya* with its negative attitude toward high society, served as models and as confirmation of Nekrasov's own tendencies in his early prose. Lermontov's prose works have left few identifiable traces of influence, since their general trend coincided with Belinsky's views of the proper function of prose.

Chernyshevsky asserted that Nekrasov was the founder of a new period of poetry. As such he was greater or "higher" than his predecessors Pushkin and Lermontov, since he realized in his poetry a higher stage of historical development. The age in which Nekrasov wrote differed, so Chernyshevsky maintained, from that of his great precursors in that the commoners had come to the forefront and had taken the lead not only in literature but in all social development. In so doing they had replaced the aristocracy and the aristocratic Decembrists. Pushkin, he continued, saw the peasant as the victim of immutable historical conditions; Lermontov saw the serfs as objects of pity who could be helped. It was Nekrasov's specific merit to see the peasant as a victim who could and should arise, throw off his fetters, and achieve freedom. This deterministic historicizing view is typical of the Chernyshevsky-Dobroliubov esthetic, and it need concern us only in so far as it had some influence on Nekrasov's own views. The poet tended to think at times in similar terms, as we have had occasion to point out in our discussion of "Sasha."

For us it is sufficient to remember that Nekrasov did indeed continue certain aspects of the tradition established by Pushkin and Lermontov, but we do not need to compare their alleged degrees of "greatness." Chernyshevsky was instinctively suspicious of all aristocrats. I. I. Panayev in his memoirs describes Lermontov as inordinately proud. He did not like to be thought of as a writer but as a man of the world. Panayev also noted the split in him between person and poet, a dissonance which he probably more readily observed since he was strongly under Belinsky's influence at the time.[6] Yet Belinsky was not blind to Lermontov's greatness. Annenkov even claims that it was Lermontov who gave Belinsky the idea that the only poetry proper to the age was that which revealed the spiritual impotence of Russia. In this respect at least Nekrasov is the direct heir of Lermontov. There are, of course, great personal differences between the poets; there are also sociological differences which we have already noted. Lermontov, where he has themes later adopted by Nekrasov, dealt with them in more Romantic form, although his sorrow and skepticism are a link with the later poetry of Nekrasov. But the accusatory pathos of Lermontov is more abstract and general than that of Nekrasov, whose poetry generally lacks the rhetorical invective of Lermontov's "The Poet" or "The Death of a Poet." Lermontov pioneered in writing poems of mixed genre with transitions in form and tone within the same poem, and in some ways poems of his such as "Sasha" or "A Tale for Children" anticipate the techniques of Nekrasov.

The split in Lermontov's personality is reflected in his view of what a poet should be. For him a poet was half popular tribune, half private skeptic. Lermontov combined these two views in his poetry in his own specific fashion, inimitable for any successor. But his longing for freedom and his sense of impotence arising out of the prevailing social conditions he shares with Nekrasov. The view of the *narod* expressed in Lermontov's late poem "The Fatherland" anticipates Nekrasov's attitudes in many respects. But in general we may say that where Lermontov is using the abstractions of Romanticism, Nekrasov has the more specific, observed detail which we call Realism. Even where they both use nearly the same language, there are notes in Nekrasov which would have been impossible in Lermontov. Both use the figure of a muse in a crown of thorns, but Nekrasov's muse whipped by a knout in public ("Yesterday at Six O'clock") could not have been written by Lermontov. Thus, Nekrasov carried further and intensified tendencies observable in Lermontov, but not dominant in his verse.

More specifically there are poems which indicate directly the influence of Lermontov. There are also, of course, those poems entitled "Imitations of Lermontov," and Nekrasov seemed to feel the urge to parody him, especially in the 1840's. Nekrasov's "Cradle Song," for example, is a deliberate parody of Lermontov's famous "Cossack Cradle Song." Lermontov's "Both Bored and Sad" supplies the first line for a Nekrasov poem which continues, however, with the words: "There's no one to cheat at cards" (I, 377). Lermontov's "They Loved Each Other so Long" becames Nekrasov's "They Went into the Tavern Together" (I, 388). The intent is the same as in the case of Pushkin, namely to poke fun at the second-rate imitators of the great poet and to attack the epigones of Romantic high style with their affectations. But aside from imitations or deliberate parodies there are other signs of Lermontov's lasting influence. In prosody Lermontov offered more than Pushkin, for while like him he preferred iambic measures, he used three-foot meters much more than Pushkin. Although anapests are rare and amphibrachs only relatively frequent, he used dactyls expertly ("The Captured Knight" or "The Clouds"), and he also employed dactylic rhymes. In rhythm and form Nekrasov's "On the Volga" is indebted to Lermontov's "The Apprentice" (1839). When Nekrasov wished to he could command the Lermontov-tone perfectly; there are even in some poems traces of Lermontov's characteristic syntax and phraseology.[7]

III *Koltsov as a Predecessor*

Krylov's fables, Ryleyev's poems of revolutionary pathos, Ogarëv's poems of melancholy and revolutionary fervor, and the broad pictures of contemporary life given by Nikitin in poems like "Taras" or "Kulak" were contributions to the treasury of Russian verse which formed Nekrasov's inheritance. But we must turn to a poet whose status as predecessor of Nekrasov is next to that of Pushkin and Lermontov. As a poet of the *narod* Koltsov is Nekrasov's most significant model. Koltsov was a pioneer in introducing into literary verse themes from village and peasant life without condescension or falsification through idealization. Anticipating Nekrasov, Koltsov wrote of peasants at work and in the fields, and not just as quaintly rustic adjuncts to the landscape. The hard lot of peasant women is a theme in some of his poems. His pictures of rural landscapes also rested on observation and were not stylized beyond recognition. Stylistically he had great influence on Nekrasov's poems in the 1840's; his use of popular speech, especially the conventional ornamental epithets, was taken over by Nekrasov in such poems as "The Gardener" and "On the Road." Traditional similes from folk speech were effectively used by Koltsov before Nekrasov had become creative in this respect and had learned to adapt or to coin his own such turns of speech. The use of popular tautologies (sad sorrow; torturing torment; wafts-blows) was quite frequent with Koltsov, and in fact he went further with this technique than did Nekrasov, who was generally more sparing in his use of such devices.

Nevertheless the vocabulary and the meters of Koltsov are very significant for Nekrasov, who continued the tendencies of Koltsov, refined and developed them, and integrated them into his own characteristic style. Dactylic rhymes are a prominent feature of Koltsov's songlike verses, a fact noted with approval by Belinsky, who was impressed with the folk-song nature of many of his poems. Belinsky was especially fond of the poems "The Harvest," "The Young Reaper," and "The Mower." In such poems Koltsov took over from folk speech the standard epithets and adjectives without changing them or stylizing them. Nekrasov tended to avoid in his mature verse those epithets and conventional attributes which contrast with everyday reality and which express an ideal or the merely wished-for. The element of wishful thinking present in popular poetry is lacking in Nekrasov. He drew many emblematic heroes, but he mixed the projection of people and things as they should be with pictures of an actual environment and portrayed possibilities of the ideal within a realistically grasped framework. His frequent visions of a better future are borne by figures idealized only to the extent that they are optimistic expressions of the potential inherent in his heroes. Important also is the fact that his heroes are those who struggle against their environment and who are critical of it, and not at peace with it like the figures of Koltsov.[8]

The differences we have just noted contributed to Dobroliubov's evaluation of Koltsov. He missed in the poet the note of protest which he considered so vital to poetry. Koltsov had themes and settings drawn from the life of the *narod,* and yet, according to Dobroliubov, he did not have a broad enough horizon, nor did he set his peasants into the framework of a larger socially conditioned setting. Therefore he considered his descriptions of folk life to be lacking in socio-historical perspective. But his view of the poet was not wholly negative. He praised Koltsov's simplicity and the lack of extraneous ornamentation in his verses. Saltykov-Shchedrin also praised his unadorned verse which achieved such fine effects and showed careful observation in the details of peasant life. He considered Koltsov not only an innovator in this field but also unequaled.

We have already mentioned Belinsky's high esteem of Koltsov. It is quite possible that Nekrasov's early interest in Koltsov may have been owing to the teaching of the great critic. It is certain, however, that Nekrasov would have discovered such a congenial poet sooner or later anyway. In 1846, together with Belinsky, Nekrasov edited and published a posthumous collection of Koltsov's poems. In 1845, while working on this edition, he wrote the poem "For that I despise Myself," published ten years later as a "translation" (I, 22). This poem is the first real echo of Koltsov in Nekrasov's poems. The four-foot anapests with rhymed couplets suggest a favorite form of Koltsov. Some turns of speech are in fact variations on lines from "The Mower" and "Russian Song" of Koltsov. Nekrasov's early skill in handling anapests may well have been learned from Koltsov. "The Gardener" has echoes of Koltsov's "The Flight"; it is one of his most Koltsovian poems. Nekrasov's favorite device of dialogue and conversations between the central figure of the poem and the narrator-poet may be found in Koltsov, although not so developed and finely nuanced as in Nekrasov. Monologues of the type found in poems like "Shyness" (1852), "Meditation" (1860), or "Kalistrat" (1863) have their prototypes in Koltsov, although it is not necessary to think of influence here, since an essential ingredient is lacking. Koltsov, as we have already noted, did not touch on the relation of peasant and serf-owner. He wrote poems in which the lyric hero is a man of the *narod* and speaks his thoughts and feelings directly to the reader, but without a note of protest. This lack of criticism is the feature which distinguished his poems from those of Nekrasov, who always emphasized the social inferiority of the serfs while suggesting their moral superiority over the serf-owners. For all the similarities then, there is one element lacking which separates Koltsov and Nekrasov as poets.

IV *Nekrasov and his Contemporaries*

Nekrasov's position among the poets of his time may be put into perspective by a comparison with Ogarëv, a poet only eight years older than Nekrasov. N. P. Ogarëv, an important publicist and revolutionary and a lifelong friend of Herzen, whose exile he shared, wrote poems on the condition of the *narod* which anticipate Nekrasov's works in subject matter and to a degree also in approach. The differences in style and musicality are marked, but the melancholy of some of his poems in the 1840's is similar to that of Nekrasov's in his penitent poems. Ogarëv is the direct heir of the Decembrist poets. It is significant that he collected and edited the poems of Ryleyev. All the contradictions and problematics of the generation succeeding the Decembrists are present in Ogarëv in exemplary form. In some ways, namely in his prosaisms, in his melancholic weariness with the world, and in his exact descriptions of his environment, Ogarëv is a precursor of Nekrasov. But in most respects their developments were parallel, and the question of influence is difficult to determine. Poems such as "The Tavern" or "The Hut," written as monologues, were at least possible models for Nekrasov. Their favorite figures and themes are very close, but presumably each developed independently. They were aware of each other's poetry, and each of them thought highly of the other, although their personal relations were clouded by quarrels.

I. I. Panayev describes Ogarëv in his memoirs as being modest, sensitive, impractical, and quite otherworldly. He was an attractive personality who had many friends.[9] His writings as a critic were important in their time, and some of his late revolutionary tracts are said to have influenced Lenin. Chernyshevsky thought very highly of him and wrote a long review of his poems in *The Contemporary* in 1856, suggesting among other things that Nekrasov was his successor.[10] His beginnings were Romantic and subjective, but under the influence of the Decembrist poets and with his maturing he turned to more serious and realistic poems. He was much attracted to the German poet Heinrich Heine, several of whose poems he translated. He especially admired Heine's satiric verse, and his translations provide a link between Heine and Nekrasov. Many of Nekrasov's characteristics are shared by

Ogarëv, whose personal presence is felt in many of his poems, but in general he always tended to be more philosophical and abstract than Nekrasov. In the early days of *The Contemporary* he was urged to contribute, although in fact very few items of his appeared in the magazine. Turgenev and L. Tolstoy admired his verses during his return to St. Petersburg in 1856; his popularity with the reading public never equaled that of Nekrasov, but he was well-known in his time as both publicist and poet, a dual role similar to that of Nekrasov. Contemporary opinion rated him highly for his skill as a versifier, but to the modern reader much of his verse seems rather mechanical. A feature of his prosody, especially in his iambic measures, is the coincidence of natural word stress with the metric accent, which results in choppy, jingly lines. Nekrasov sometimes wrote this way to achieve comic effects in his satiric verse.

With so much in common and with a contemporary reputation among the intellectuals of the period that was approximately the same, one might well ask how they differed and how posterity has nearly forgotten the poet (but not the publicist) Ogarëv while raising Nekrasov to a position of fame. Chernyshevsky points in passing to one cause when he mentions the historical conditioning of Ogarëv, who grew up in an age when there was no alternative to autocracy and when literature was solely for the intelligentsia. Ogarëv wrote his poems for the intelligentsia, for people of similar background and learning to his own, even when taking his themes from the contemporary scene. His poems about peasant life and conditions are obviously written from the spectator's point of view. But most important of all, he created no great poetic figures comparable to Nekrasov's Vlas, Sasha, the grandfather Decembrist, or the Russian princesses. Although many of his poems are of high quality; there is no genre which he developed to the point of excellence beyond that of his contemporaries; and there is no specific quality of excellence which we can praise as unique and peculiar to him alone.

Nekrasov's contemporaries tended to link his name with that of Ogarëv and to see them as peers. But we must note the fact that most of Nekrasov's contemporary critics among his fellow writers failed to see Nekrasov's greatness. We naturally except close friends like Chernyshevsky and Dobroliubov, and we must discount their opinions too, since they often praised him for his ideology rather than for his artistic achievements. Nineteenth-century praise of Nekrasov is as suspect as the criticism is insensitive. The Popularists, for example, considered his didactic and accusatory poems the greatest of the century. But they were either totally oblivious to his artistic merits or viewed his art as minor and secondary. Plekhanov, in an article in 1903, emphasized the revolutionary influence of Nekrasov, especially on the youth of his time, but combined this praise with condescending remarks about his poetic language. He also found Nekrasov's poetry to be not nearly aggressive enough, claiming that it led more to patient suffering than to action. This essay, with both its insights and its errors, played an important role in early Soviet views of Nekrasov. Later Soviet critics usually polemicize against it.

Druzhinin, a close friend of Turgenev, at first hardly mentioned Nekrasov. But since in the 1850's Nekrasov was very popular with the reading public, he began to refer to him, usually contenting himself with oblique reproaches of didacticism and tendentiousness. Turgenev considered Tiutchev the greatest poet of his time; he thought Nekrasov on a par with Fet and Maikov. Nekrasov for his part not only thought very highly of Turgenev but also loved him as a friend whom he addressed with the intimate "thou." Even while they were close friends and collaborators, Turgenev did not hide his dislike of Nekrasov's poetry. We have mentioned certain early poems which Turgenev liked; in general, however, he considered Nekrasov a minor poet full of prosy lines. In a letter to Polonsky he referred to Nekrasov as a poet full of strain and bits and pieces whose verse amounted to chewed papier-mâché with a sprinkling of bitter vodka.[11] This was written after the break with Nekrasov and *The Contemporary*, and personal bitterness plays a part in the harsh judgment. The critical opinions of writers at that period did not prevent them from various forms of collaboration, however, and for years Nekrasov and Turgenev worked together, even editing in cooperation an edition of Fet's poems. In the early 1850's, Fet visited at the hospitable Panayev home, reading his poems to the usual group at the house. Both Turgenev and Nekrasov admired Fet's verses, but Fet was always quite condescending toward Nekrasov as a poet, sharing the low opinion of Turgenev, Botkin, Annenkov, and Druzhinin.

Nekrasov, who was not only sensitive and perceptive in his judgments of other writers, but also basically tolerant and generous, fared poorly at the hands of his friends and contemporaries. He was enshrined in the hearts of the public long before he was accepted at full value by the arbiters of art and criticism; it is really only during the Soviet period that an appreciation of him consistent with his achievements has become general. Ogarëv, in so many ways a kindred spirit, was one of the few contemporary writers who saw the true function of his poetry and appreciated both his art and his place in history.[12] A. Grigor'ev, who did not like Nekrasov's didactic and preaching poems, did admit his positive qualities and ranked him with Koltsov, Turgenev, and Ostrovsky. In the 1860's, seeking to place him in historical perspective, he connected Nekrasov above all with Pushkin, secondarily with Lermontov and Koltsov, thus achieving an anticipation of the modern view.

V *Evaluations of Nekrasov*

Much of the failure to see Nekrasov's greatness and to appreciate his position as the great continuer of the poetic tradition founded by Pushkin and Lermontov is because of a misunderstanding of his style and choice of lexical levels. Even modern critics are bemused by his prosaisms, his use of popular speech, and even vulgarisms in his satiric verses. It is easy and traditional to overemphasize these features of his poetry. It is true, however, that he was an innovator in the use of the language of business, with words like career, credit, series, or bank note and benefits, all of which appear in "Contemporaries." The conversational tones in his narrative diction, sometimes spiced with journalistic phrases, have led critics to speak of his "lowering" the level of poetic language and using an "inferior" style.[13] The changes in style and tonality within the same poem have brought the reproach of impurity of genre in his verses. His constant protesting has been a stumbling block for those who believe that such tendencies are by nature unpoetic, and we must admit that some poems have an overemphasis in this respect.

Overlooked in such assessments is a basic fact which forms the core of Chukovsky's excellent study of Nekrasov, namely that the poet always used that specific style which was uniquely appropriate to the subject matter and the intent of the particular poem.[14] Shifts in style and lexical level are possible where the dominant tone of a poem is capable of blending such changes into the whole. And it is in this skill of blending that Nekrasov is unexcelled; those transitions which are still felt as breaks in style are deliberate and mark off sections of a particular poem and a shift either of subject or of attitude toward it. The reader may test this for himself in a poem like "The Railroad," where there is a neutral, narrative style, the voice of a child, ecstatic vision, ironized tones from the general, satiric effects in the description of the petty exploiters, humor, pathos, subtle counterpoint and careful composition, and all this wide range is balanced and woven together into an artistic whole. Changes in style and tone are not necessarily defects; they may serve to enrich a poem with variations and nuances in diction as well as in such formal aspects as rhyme and meter. Nekrasov's use of changes in formal respects such as length of line and change of meter may be observed in all their subtlety and skill in poems like "Red-nosed Frost," where, for example, the emphatic short line often precedes a shift in the narrative perspective. If we admit the possibility of a mixed genre in which narration, description, and dialogue with dramatic scenes are all permissible, then we may conclude that Nekrasov mastered this form in his longer poems.

But it is not only in his longer, narrative poems that we find traits which are either innovations or continuations of that part of the Pushkin legacy overlooked or rejected by his contemporaries. As a poet of nature Nekrasov has few equals. The special quality of those passages in his poems which conjure up the Russian landscape is due to several factors. Most of his descriptions are remarkable for their specific, sharply observed details. The primacy of people over objects, however, is always present as a compositional principle, so that these details never exist for themselves, but only as the precise setting for human beings with their joys and sorrows. The poem "Knight for an Hour" is one of the striking examples of this feature of his poetry. In this poem the attention to nature and the descriptions of intimate details are used to organize the poet's mixed feelings, and the descriptions accompany the waverings of his emotions as he tries to escape his emotional urges or overcome them, or yields to the melancholy of memory.

But of course the feelings of sorrow and self-reproach are not the only ones associated with the pictures of nature. In "The Green Sound" the harmony of life and its connection with the changing seasons, especially the joy of springtime, are a cause for rejoicing and enjoyment. The sights and sounds of nature are for man's pleasure and spiritual comfort. Closest to nature is the peasant who tills the soil; the favorite figure from peasant life is for Nekrasov the plowman. Peasants who worked in the fields seemed to the poet to have a "natural" growth and health in consonance with nature, and in this he delighted. He took pleasure in natural beauty for its own sake, but more often and typically he used the beauties of nature as a contrast to the sorry condition of mankind. One of his most striking uses of nature for this purpose is to be found in the opening lines of "The Railroad."

A large part of the poet's enduring fame rests on his famous portraits of women. Here better than in any other respect he may be easily set apart from his contemporaries, none of whom equaled him. He continued the tradition of *Eugene Onegin* in making his feminine figures at once both representative and individual. He rarely wrote in the abstract about womankind, or generalized about some undefined and unvisualizable beloved, but created contoured figures with recognizable traits and personality. The economy of effort with which he produced these figures was unparalleled in his time. The concision and compactness with which he is able to make even minor figures come alive in his verses is brilliantly illustrated in "Russian Women." Even when a general type is the subject of the poem, as is the case in "At the Height of the Harvest," in which any peasant woman might be meant, intimate details and close observation make the total picture vivid. Dramatic effects in scenes that could easily be acted out recur in his poems frequently; dramatic dialogues were developed far beyond anything since *Eugene Onegin.*

Not only in his famous portraits of Russian women, but in all his verse there is a constant tension between two complementary forces. On the one hand Nekrasov sought to suggest, particularly in his portraits of people, the broadest representative qualities. He endowed his figures with individual traits, but at the same time gave them a setting and function that was typified. On the other hand, especially in his descriptions of nature and of objects, he strove for the most precise details. These two strivings reinforce each other. Sometimes the urge to achieve the specific detail leads to prosiness, as for example in the use of exact numbers which are often startling in their unexpected context. These prosaisms were unusual and disconcerting for his contemporaries. A poem that begins "Yesterday at six o'clock" suggests a reporter's narrative, not a poem of pity and pathos. But in his striving for typical qualities, especially in drawing his emblematic heroes, he did not hesitate to achieve a generalizing effect by the use of abstract language. He spoke, when he considered it apposite, of Love, Faith, Hope, Work, Truth, Freedom, and Service, capitalizing the nouns for emphasis. His broad range of tones included the language of high rhetoric as well as the turns of popular speech or the jargon of journalism. He was careful to fit his language to the person speaking or being spoken of; his characterization by the use of language is often very subtle. In his serious poems, but not in his satire, he frequently indicated the social level of the speaker and assigned personal speech forms by the use of varying syntactical constructions rather than by a choice of vocabulary. There are notable exceptions to this general rule, and in those passages where he speaks as author-narrator the lexical choice covers the full range from near-dialect to solemnly archaic words of Church Slavonic form. And again and again he returned to condensation and concision as the means of lending emphasis to his message. It is not surprising then that the most famous quotations from his poems are largely aphoristic.[15]

The path of an innovator is seldom smooth. The difficulty in assessing Nekrasov's proper worth arose from a misunderstanding of very personal developments which are innovations only to the extent that the emphasis and personal tone color was new. As we have pointed out in our discussion of Nekrasov's relations to his predecessors, a precedent can be found for almost everything which Nekrasov undertook. But it was difficult for his contemporaries to see those basic aspects of his work which represent a consistent continuation of the classic tradition, and their misunderstandings have survived over the years and have been repeated often enough to become clichés of criticism. Madame Jarintsov, seeking to characterize briefly his poetic production, mentions his poems about cabmen, carters, gardeners, printers, soldiers, hawkers, prostitutes, convicts, and peasants, and his descriptions of street scenes, fires, funerals, tragic weddings, cruel dissipation, the vulgarities and platitudes of town life, and the corruption of officialdom.[16] If one lists his subjects in this bald fashion, it seems obvious enough that Nekrasov does not stand in the Olympian tradition. He provided Russian verse with a new melody, broadening the scope of what was acceptable as "poetic" and enlarging the horizons of literary verse. Nekrasov was the boldest of his period in creating new genres, mixtures of genres, combining political verses with confessional lyrics, satirical chronicles with revolutionary poems with a historical base, and vignettes of mixed dramatic and lyric effects. The synthesis of the social and the intimately personal in his verse meant an enrichment of the possibilities of poetry. In prosody too he had a great influence. Until his time, with the exception of Koltsov, the folk-meters, trochaic rhythm with dactyls at the end of the metric line, were infrequently used in literary verse. Nekrasov's success with these meters marks an enrichment of the accepted forms in Russian versification. It is true, however, that his example was not always a happy one for those who came after him. Those of his imitators who adopted the metrical scheme of "Russian Women," with its short lines and deceptively simple metrical pattern, tended to produce jingly verse. The successors of Nekrasov have been accused of writing "flat and anemic poetry." [17]

VI *Nekrasov's Successors*

Nekrasov's successors tended to imitate all aspects of his poetry, but it is usually only in satire that it is customary to speak of the "Nekrasov tendency" as a synonym for poetry of social criticism or "citizen poetry." [18] The best known satirists who came under his influence are Kurochkin, Saltykov-Shchedrin, and Minaev.[19] Nekrasov's satiric verses had a great vogue during the 1860's and 1870's, which was an age of the flowering of satire in Russia. Satiric periodicals like *The Spark* enjoyed an even higher circulation than *The Contemporary*. Satire was an outlet for all those who were dissatisfied with the conditions of the country, regardless of their political views. Even Fet, a conservative who considered Nekrasov a pseudo-poet who catered to the whims of the masses, wrote some political verses. Maikov, usually ranked among the "pure poets," also wrote topical verses. Even A. K. Tolstoy, an aristocrat and by no means a radical, collaborated with two of his cousins under the pseudonym of Koz'ma Prutkov to write satires which were published in the supplement to *The Contemporary*, "The Whistle." Among the targets of his satire were the estheticism of the pure poets, the Romanticism of some contemporaries (including parodies of Fet), and the complacency of the educated Philistines. At precisely the same time the poems of K. K. Sluchevsky, a gifted younger member of the advocates of pure poetry, were published in *The Contemporary*.[20]

There is a school of thought which rejects the terms "citizen poetry" and "pure poetry" as inadequate and misleading, since pure poetry is a myth on the one hand, and on the other some "political" poets, like Nekrasov, wrote subjective lyrics as well as tendentious poetry. The differences between the schools of poetry lie mainly in their political attitudes and allegiance, rather than in the actual poetic practice. We have used the terms as useful labels, however, and they are traditional in speaking of the period in question. But we have mentioned the poems of Fet and Maikov, and the satire of A. K. Tolstoy both as a warning against oversimplification and as a supplement to the one-sided picture that might emerge if one deals only with the theory of the era.

It is also easy to exaggerate the importance of Nekrasov's conflicts with his contemporaries and the prolonged polemics of *The Contemporary*. As an editor Nekrasov seems to have led a life of uninterrupted forensic jousts. In spite of all appearances to the contrary Nekrasov was not really always tendentious; as a poet he expressed the thoughts and feelings which were dear to him—protest was part of his nature—but the accusations of preaching, thrown at him by so many of his contemporaries, do not really concern his nonsatiric verse. As a critic he was opposed to mere tendentiousness. Eloquent testimony for this may be found in his treatment of writers like Pisemsky, whom he rebuked for his heaping up of sordid facts. Part of his quarrel with Pisarev arises from the same source. He was opposed to vulgar realism, and impatient with "realistic" details that seemed to be an end by themselves and were not illumined by some idea. For this reason he did not rate Charles Dickens very highly, preferring, if the choice must be made, the Romanticism of a George Sand, in whom he believed he felt great warmth and sincerity. Even though he believed that literature should have a lucid and logical ideational basis, he distinguished the fundamental idea or point of view of a poem from the form of its expression, rejecting mere propaganda or obvious preaching. In this connection we may refer back to his concept of the freedom of the artist: a tendentious writer starts with a slant; a great writer begins with inspiration and ideas that arise "freely." The constraint and compulsion of prejudice or ideology were anathema to him. By writing well one serves both literature and society, for by serving literature fully one inevitably also serves society.[21]

Nekrasov was primarily a practitioner; he never developed a theory of poetry, nor did he seek to buttress his writing with philosophical speculations. As a poet he was an innovator who seemed to overturn the old esthetic canons of poetry, but as a theorist he never established a poetics nor made any attempt to formulate his ideas on poetry in essayistic fashion. He was not an abstract thinker but a poet most at ease with visual images. His letters contain the scattered fragments of a poetics, and from the reviews and the poems themselves we can deduce some of his esthetic beliefs.[22] But in a way it would seem that he never really accepted his own poetry in the light of a firm philosophical and theoretical position. In part his severe and hypercritical self-depreciation accounts for this seeming paradox. Even up to his last days he felt that he had failed as person and as poet.

His sense of failure was not shared by the reading public. And it was not shared either by many poets who became, in some degree, his successors and the continuers of the tradition he had established.[23] Among those who show a good deal of affinity with Nekrasov we may mention A. N. Pleshcheyev (1825–93), I. S. Nikitin,[24] and M. L. Mikhailov. Especially in the case of the last-named poet it is debatable to what degree he was influenced by Nekrasov; it is more likely that he was a congenial product of the *Zeitgeist*. Nekrasov's influence on like-minded writers can easily be exaggerated, especially if one forgets that much of what Nekrasov was doing was in the popular current of his times that swept along others as well. The radical intelligentsia consisted of differentiated individuals with common concerns. Since Nekrasov is the greatest poet of the group it is easy to assign to him what was in fact common property. His distinctive contribution is to be sought in his art, not in his ideology. The interest of the Soviet poets in Nekrasov has naturally been shaped by their ideological convictions; his satire and prosodic practice have been the facets of his writing that have exerted the greatest appeal.

VII *The Rediscovery of Nekrasov*

We have dealt at some length with the problem of Nekrasov's evaluation by contemporary writers in order to give the reader some perspective for a view of the nineteenth century. Not yet discussed is how it came about that Nekrasov was finally admitted to the pantheon guarded zealously by the critics and the historians. The rediscovery of Nekrasov as an artist and master of poetry begins with the Symbolists.[25] Their critical evaluations of him opened the way for later assessments which could appreciate his genuine qualities as a poet. The Symbolists can hardly be said to have imitated him, but they were intrigued by his ability to make poetry out of everyday and commonplace life and by the poetic harmony he created in poems about harsh reality. There is little in Balmont or Blok that recalls Nekrasov's poetics, but the Symbolists were aware of Nekrasov's techniques and were the first literary group to appreciate his prosody.[26]

More important, however, and contributing more directly to the modern view is another literary circle of the twentieth century. Russian Formalism arose about 1914, was suppressed by the government in 1930, and had its greatest flowering in the 1920's.[27] The Formalists evaluated positively what many of Nekrasov's contemporaries had viewed with alarm, namely, the influence on his poetic diction of the vocabulary and idioms of vaudeville farces and journalistic language. In a way they admired Nekrasov for the very faults which were considered so damaging by earlier schools of thought. In correcting past errors they sometimes went too far; Eikhenbaum, for example, overemphasizes Nehrasov's tendency to "lower" the lexical level of his verse and puts too much stress on what he considers the "deliberate disharmony" in his poems. He views these tendencies positively, approving them as valuable innovations, thereby very nearly arriving at a misunderstanding equal and opposite to that of Nekrasov's contemporaries. Yet his chapter in the book *On Literature* (1924) is the first modern attempt to deal seriously with Nekrasov's diction and his versification, and it is an invaluable contribution to the study of Nekrasov. Later Soviet critics owe much to it, although their debt is usually unacknowledged, since officially the Formalists have been in disfavor since 1930 and a conspiracy of silence surrounds them. Until the middle 1920's Nekrasov's admirers praised his civic poetry for its social message, but they also agreed with his detractors that formally Nekrasov was a weak and clumsy versifier.

The Formalist break with the traditional views of the poet prepared the way for the Soviet critics. Their silent debt to the Formalists was a mixed blessing, however, since the notion that Nekrasov had written in a hybrid style compounded of Pushkinisms and folk songs persisted effectively until Chukovsky's *The Mastery of Nekrasov.* Since the mid-1950's, spurred on by the publication at long last of a definitive edition with variant readings, Soviet scholarship may point with pride to great achievements. Soviet scholars have earned the world's gratitude for their painstaking research and success in establishing a definitive text, collecting his letters and autobiographical fragments, ascertaining the details of his life, and contributing special studies which have made clear his sources, many parallels, and other data essential to an understanding of the poet. Their studies of his vocabulary, his folklore sources (collections of fairy tales and proverbs), and of the historical allusions and references in his works have refashioned completely the scholarly view of Nekrasov and have opened the way for comprehensive interpretations. In effect they have presented the world with a new great poet.

Soviet scholars have certain special interests in Nekrasov which are secondary for foreigners, but which are met with so frequently and which recur so insistently that they deserve passing mention. Since they have adopted him as a precursor of the Revolution, it is natural that they read into him proto-Marxist ideas in order to fit him into their historical scheme. They repeat to the point of tedium the statement that he loved the serfs and hated their oppressors, and praise him (often in lieu of analyzing his verse) for his progressive, democratic, radical, and revolutionary ideas. These are all good words in the Soviet vocabulary. The earlier Soviet critics, before the Second World War, tended to underscore the fact that he had indeed held a historical place in Russian letters, but since he lived before the gospel according to Marx and Lenin, he was subject to errors and transgressions and may even have been tempted by deviations such as Utopian Socialism, a dreadful aberration. Postwar critics do not spare their own Soviet predecessors corrective criticism, and they usually begin by either refuting or placing in proper perspective the first generation of Soviet critics. They now insist on Nekrasov's orthodoxy, on his intuitive anticipation of later Communist doctrines, and extend their hagiography backwards in time.

All of this would be only mildly annoying if it did not affect the image of Nekrasov as a figure of great stature in Russian literature and consequently also a figure of world literature. Much of the difficulty in reworking and explicating the poet's position stems from problems such as his attitude towards the emancipation of the serfs. He and his like-minded friends scoffed at it and the reforms which followed and accompanied it. But the reforms were necessary in order to transform Russia from a country with an agrarian economy based on serfdom to a "modern" country with an industrial economy. A necessary historical stage in the development of industry in the nineteenth century was capitalism, which could not develop under the system of serfdom. Capitalism was necessary for the growth of a proletariat which would then arise, take over control, and usher in the socialist millennium. Thus the credo. In the series of deterministic historical stages the Emancipation appears as a necessity, as a positive step in the right direction. To oppose it means to oppose forces of history which are right, inevitable and part of the rigid doctrine. (The Soviets now believe that industrialization can be achieved through "social" accumulation.)

Yet Nekrasov is quite rightly a hero of the Revolution. His writings did more to help the revolutionary cause than those of any other major literary figure. The memoirs of active revolutionaries document this again and again. We have the testimony of Madame Krupskaya (Lenin's wife) that Lenin read Nekrasov while in exile; Lenin knew Nekrasov so well that he quoted his verses from memory. Almost all Soviet critics are able to cite Lenin positively on the subject of Nekrasov.[28] There is, of course, no possibility of quarreling with Lenin's opinions, which are as sacred and inviolable as any Vedic hymn and have the force of revelation. The difficulty lies in reconciling his high opinion of Nekrasov with the facts. Much ingenuity has been spent on this problem. No reader of Soviet secondary literature will be spared passages of polemics and explications that deal with this issue. We may safely ignore all this otiose casuistry and be content with the fact that Nekrasov is the greatest poet of the mid-century in Russia and has a claim to world fame far beyond that which he has enjoyed up to now.

Notes and References

Chapter One

1. All the translations from the Russian are our own. We must apologize here for their inadequacy. They do not render the musicality or the tone color of the original Russian, nor do they imitate the rhyme or rhythm. They are merely attempts to give, in rhythmic prose where possible, the basic sense of what Nekrasov said so much better.

2. The Statutes of February 19, 1861 (22 separate enactments) filled 360 pages. We are indebted to Professor Peter Czap of the Amherst College History Department for the following summary. The "General Regulations on Peasants Emerging from Bondage" began: "The enserfment of peasants is forever abolished . . . [and former serfs] are granted by right the status of free rural inhabitants, personally and with respect to property." What follows deals with peasant land tenure and was more or less equally applied throughout the Empire. These rules applied only to those peasants who were elegible to receive land; no provision was made to provide land for the former household serfs (*dvorovye*), nor could they become members of rural communes, and thus gain a share of land, without the consent of the commune. There were several million *dvorovye* who were left in legal limbo.

I. Within one year after emancipation, estate owners were required to prepare an inventory (*ustavnaya gramota*) listing land actually in possession of the peasants (i.e., their huts and plowland) and the *barshchina* and/or *obrok* (*corvée* and payment in lieu of service) due for it. If landowners failed to draw up an inventory it was done by a "peace arbitrator" (*mirovoi posrednik*). Within two years after emancipation these inventories were to be presented to the peasants (any differencs of opinion between peasants and former owners were to be mediated by peace arbitrators) and then officially introduced as the basis of economic relations between peasants and former owners. Thus, on February 19, 1863, Phase I of the emancipation ended with the entire peasant population regulated according to *ustavnye gramoty* and designated "temporarily obliged" peasants.

II. Phase II was the "redemption" phase. First, however, the following should be kept in mind about temporary obligation. No time limit was set for the period of temporary obligation; the government specified only that in 1881 the *ustavnye gramoty* should be revised. The peasants could not terminate the period of temporary obligation; this could only be done by the bilateral action of peasants and estate owner or unilaterally by the estate owner. (In 1883 the government forced all landlords who had not done so to embark on the redemption phase.) The redemption debt to be assumed by the peasants for the land which was to be transferred to them was arrived at by capitalizing at 6 per cent the annual charges assessed on that land according to the *ustavnaya gramota*. Thus, Phase II of the emancipation ended when peasants and landlords agreed on the precise amount and price of land to be deeded to the peasants. (During the period of temporary obligation all land belonged to the landowner.) Phase II was completed by some peasants as early as 1863, and by some not until 1883.

III. The third phase was the period of amortization of debt. Landlords were advanced by the government interest-bearing bonds to the amount of 80 per cent of the total indemnification to which they were entitled; the remaining 20 per cent was to be paid them directly by the peasants. The peasants in turn repaid the government the money (i.e., the value of the bonds) it advanced to the landlords, *plus interest*, in annual installments for *49 years*. Fulfillment of this obligation ended Phase III and peasants received clear title to the land.

Further comments: In general the "redemption value" of land deeded to the peasants was often several times higher than the market value of that land. In many cases peasants could not earn on a piece of land in a year enough money to pay the annual redemption payments. Another important point is that the land was deeded not to individual peasants, but to village communes which were recognized as legal corporate entities and were responsible for discharging all the obligations within the community as it saw fit and enforcing its will. Thus the argument was made that the paternal authority once exercised by the serf-owner over the serf was transferred to the peasant commune. The government hit upon this scheme in order to secure its tax base, believing that a commune was more reliable than an individual.

Another side to the emancipation is the legal status of the

peasantry. The General Regulations created a new department in the Ministry of the Interior in which all local administration of the peasantry was concentrated (distinct from the administration of nonpeasants). Furthermore, peasants were largely excluded from the general judicial system. Thus, although peasants ceased to be chattels and became "citizens," they became second-class citizens. This situation did not change until 1889, when the peasants became third-class citizens.

3. Cf. IX, 78; 93–94; 156; 159; X, 232; 240; 283–84.

4. These topical themes appealed greatly to the *raznochintsy*, and led to the great cult of Gogol, who was widely and avidly read, even learned by heart.

Chapter Two

1. These are now available in the *Complete Works and Letters;* there are also further details and commentary in the biography of Evgen'ev-Maksimov.

2. Cf. VI, 559; 562.

3. E.g. IX, 12; 18.

4. IX, 453; XII, 12.

5. Cf. IX, 13; 43; 56; 81.

6. Cf. IX, 453; 503; 523; 532.

7. E.g., the reviews of Fet, Maikov, and Polonsky: IX, 273; 279; 393.

8. Cf. IX, 180–81.

9. Cf. XII, 105.

10. Cf. IX, 344; 369.

11. Cf. X, 247f.; 259; IX, 293.

12. Cf. IX, 142.

13. Dostoyevsky, F. M. *The Diary of a Writer.* Translated by Boris Brasol. New York: George Braziller, 1954. In pages 585f. he describes his "discovery" by the Belinsky-group, tells how Grigorovich and Nekrasov woke him out of bed to acclaim his *Poor Folk.*

14. Poems on censorship, or which refer to it: "V. G. Belinsky" (1855); "The Reading Room" (1865); "Recent Times" (1871); and "Songs of the Free Word" (the "new law on censorship" was issued 6 April, 1865).

15. Chukovsky, K. *The Mastery of Nekrasov,* p. 100.

16. The 1850's were a period of rapid growth in journalism. From 1851 to 1855 only 30 new periodicals appeared, but between 1856 and 1860 the total number had risen to about 150 magazines and newspapers.

17. The story of the purchase is a short novel by itself. Interesting details may be found in K. Chukovsky's *Books and People,* p. 18 f. Cf. also X, 53.

18. Letter to Botkin of 11 April, 1847 (X, 66f.).

19. *The Contemporary* was founded by Pushkin in 1836. After his death P. A. Pletnëv, professor at the University of St. Petersburg, took over the magazine. In the 1840's under his editorship the magazine never had over 400 subscribers. Under Nekrasov the magazine had 2,000 subscribers in 1847, and 3,100 in 1848. After this the numbers varied from year to year, reaching over 7,000 at times, dropping back whenever censorship pressure became too great. Cf. Evgen'ev-Maksimov, *Creative Career,* p. 101.

20. Cf. IX, 135. Evgen'ev-Maksimov, *loc. cit.,* p. 116.

21. *Literary Heritage,* III, 474 f.

22. Chukovsky, *Books and People,* p. 341 f.

23. In the 1860's there were several Slavophil periodicals, the best-known being *Russian Conversation, Fame, The Sail,* and *Day.* Conservative periodicals were among others: *Reading Library* (edited by Druzhinin; after his death by Pisemsky); Krayevsky's *Notes of the Fatherland;* and Katkov's *Russian Messenger.* Among those periodicals closer in tendency to *The Contemporary* were: *Russian Word,* edited by D. I. Pisarev; the satiric magazine *The Spark;* and Herzen's London-published *The Bell.*

24. The extent to which she contributed and the sections assigned primarily to her may be checked in Evgen'ev-Maksimov's biography.

25. The memoirs of Antonovich, Mikhailovsky, Pypin, and Kovalevsky have been used by Soviet critics to refute the rumors that circulated for years and were often carelessly repeated.

26. *N. A. Dobroliubov's Selected Philosophical Essays,* translated by J. Feinberg, Moscow, 1956.

27. Tolstoy and Turgenev could not stand each other either. Madame Panayeva's salon was the scene of some of their bitterest quarrels.

28. The following figures on peasant revolts (official figures) may help to clarify the general picture of unrest: 1865, 25; 1857, 40; 1858, 86; 1859, 90; 1860, 108; 1861, 1,176; 1862, 400; 1863, 386; 1864, 75; 1865, 93; 1866, 70.

29. Cf. "The Enemy Rejoices," II, 255.

30. The article in question was "On National Education," 1874.

31. "Every Russian writer was made conscious that he was on a public stage, testifying; so that the smallest lapse on his part, a lie, a deception, an act of self-indulgence, lack of zeal for the truth, was a heinous crime. . . . But if you spoke in public at all, be it as poet or novelist or historian or in whatever public capacity, then you accepted

full responsibility for guiding and leading the people." "A Marvellous Decade," in *Encounter*, IV, 36. Isaiah Berlin's essay on the 1840's is highly recommended reading.

Chapter Three

1. For further details consult A. M. Garkavi's article in *Nekrasov Collection* I, 150 f.

2. One of the principles applied in the composition of the book was that of alternation of types of poems, but the partly subjective, partly political reasons for the positioning of the poems are no longer fruitful to follow. Modern editions usually either arrange in chronological order his "verses," that is, the shorter poems, and then his "poémy," the longer, narrative poems, or resort to a simple, unclassified chronological sequence. Since most of Nekrasov's poems may be assigned to several categories at once, it is necessary to make arbitrary groupings for the purpose of discussion.

3. Nekrasov always visualized his muse as a robust young peasant woman. Cf. XII, 25. But he also thought of Russia as a woman; perhaps the flogged peasant woman is a symbol of Mother Russia.

4. In Russian, "high style" means in large part a choice of lexical levels. There are in Russian very often two words that are near synonoms, one Church Slavonic, the other purely Russian. This is more than an etymological distinction, because the associations with the two words will differ. The Church Slavonic word is usually felt to be more "poetic," slightly archaic often too, and thus it belongs to "high style." For example, "lukavy" is biblical-poetic for "khitry," and "duma" is more poetic than "mysl'," or "usta" than "guby." An old word may be a folk usage, however, in contrast to learned language, e.g., "volia" is in Nekrasov's time the peasant word for "svoboda" (freedom).

5. Cf. *Dead Souls*, Book One, Chapter Seven.

6. *Russian Poets and Poems*, p. 257.

7. Unbegaun, p. 46.

8. *Diary of a Writer*, p. 803.

9. His earliest poem on this topic is "For That I Despise Myself," 1845.

10. *Continuity and Change in Russian and Soviet Thought*, article by Rufus Mathewson, p. 255 f. "The Hero and Society." Page 256: "The 'superfluous man' was ironically intended as a hero of his time. And the 'new man' thought up by the radical democrats between 1855 and 1865 to replace him in life and literature, represented a return to the explicitly virtuous, emblematic men of earlier forms." He goes on to point out that the *bogatyri*, the emblematic heroes were not realistic portraits, but models, "not representing living men or observed be-

havior, but supposed to illustrate a design for life as it should be . . ." He adds that the positive political hero has his origin in the utilitarian esthetic developed by Chernyshevsky.

Chapter Four

1. Ovsianikov-Kulikovsky, p. 293. "Sasha" is also included in the poems listed as among his best.
2. Nekrasov knew this attitude very well. In "Sasha" he wrote ironically: "Learning frightens the village mind."
3. Publication in *The Bell* is an interesting fact by itself, since the periodical rarely published verse, and at just this time the personal relations between Nekrasov and Herzen were very strained.
4. In a formal sense there is no cycle of his poems on peasant themes, which are scattered among his other poems. The grouping is that of the author of this book.
5. Cf. *Nekrasov Collection* I, 68–69; 86–101.
6. Until 1874 peasants were drafted for 25 years of service. Corporal punishment was widely used. Enlisted men were at the mercy of the officers' caprice.
7. Mirsky, p. 302.
8. Dobroliubov's article is entitled "The Degree of Participation of the *Narod* in Russian Literature."
9. Cf. IX, 139.
10. This interpretation, which we do not wish to insist on, is based on A. V. Popov's article "Folklore in the Poem 'The Pedlars,'" *Nekrasov Collection* III, 86 f.
11. Students interested in the prosody of the poem may consult F. I. Evnin's article "On the Poem 'Red-nosed Frost,'" *Nekrasov Collection* III, 59 f.
12. While this is indeed a hallmark of his verse in its specific quality, other writers of course, such as Turgenev in his *Sportsman's Notes,* achieved a similar combination.

Chapter Five

1. XI, 332.
2. XI, 208.
3. Prince Trubetskoi, chosen as the leader of the uprising, did not actually appear in the Senate Square for the revolt itself. This astonishing fact was obviously not utilized by Nekrasov. The poet did not know that Princess Volkonskaya's father had died before she left for Siberia.
4. *Diary of a Writer*, p. 80.
5. Chukovsky, *Mastery*, p. 242 f. Although Chukovsky has a very sound grasp of Nekrasov's working methods, in this case he is carried

away by the notion that Nekrasov was stylizing solely in the direction of heroics.

6. Cf. the article by T. A. Besedina in *Nekrasov Collection* III, 113 f.

Chapter Six

1. Pares, *Russian Verse*, introduction, p. xxix.
2. This section and the following quotations are from *Diary of a Writer*, p. 937 f.
3. Cf. IX, 344, 364, 369.
4. Cf. IX, 191.
5. *The Poets of Russia*, p. 30: "Lermontov is perhaps the most subjective of all Russian poets, the one most concerned with his own ego, with his own selfhood."
6. *Literary Memoirs*, p. 137.
7. For further details and specific data the student may consult B. M. Eikhenbaum's *On Literature*, p. 263 f.
8. Savely, the "All-Russian hero" of "Who Can Be Happy in Russia?" is pictured at the end as broken and subdued—a bit of honest realism.
9. *Literary Memoirs*, p. 272.
10. Now in Chernyshevsky's *Collected Works*, Vol. III.
11. Letter of 13 January, 1868, to Ia. P. Polonsky.
12. Ogarëv, N. P. *Selected Works*, Moscow, 1956, II, 497.
13. Even a critic sensitive to stylistic nuances such as Eikhenbaum overemphasizes Nekrasov's urge to lower the stylistic level of verse and bring it nearer to prose. He refers to Nekrasov's desire to establish a feeling for dissonance and disharmony: *On Literature*, pp. 242–43. In general he viewed Nekrasov's style as a mixture of Pushkin-Lermontov elements with the motifs and rhythms of vaudeville, or with folk songs —a formula which is true enough, but misleading unless carefully used; Chukovsky has done much to make the formula more precise and meaningful by demonstrating just how and when he used various elements of style. Ovsianikov-Kulikovsky, a great believer in psychological types and the psychological approach to literature, concedes that Nekrasov was "completely independent and original as a folk-poet and as a mourner of the people's sorrows," p. 319, ignoring with this remark the importance of poets like Koltsov. He goes on to characterize Nekrasov as very intelligent, but also very practical, with the mind of a politician. He considers him realistic and sober in his cast of thought but denies that he was a genius or truly creative.
14. *Mastery*, p. 217 f. In making his very convincing case Chukovsky goes into great detail, more than we can permit ourselves here. Obviously the question of a "style appropriate to the theme" is a matter of

judgment from case to case. Cf. II, 439: "Important in a poem is a style corresponding to the theme." And: "Let the words be compact and the ideas spacious."

15. *Ibid.*, p. 299f.

16. Jarintzov, p. 258.

17. Erlich, p. 18.

18. Lest the reader be confused by different terminologies occasionally used, it should be said that the "Nekrasov School" of poets, not necessarily just satirists, is considered to include Dobroliubov, Nikitin, Durochkin, Minaev, Mikhailov and Pleshcheyev, and sometimes now also Ogarëv.

19. Egolin, p. 225 f.

20. He was published on the recommendation of Turgenev. Some of his poems were immediately parodied by Dobroliubov, who was amused by their remoteness from any possible reality.

21. X, 247 (Letter to V. P. Botkin of 16 September, 1855).

22. The letters of 1855–56, especially those to L. Tolstoy, are among the best sources.

23. Further details may be found in the summations of A. M. Egolin, *loc. cit.*

24. Cf. IX, 294. Nekrasov did not approve everything that Nikitin wrote. In one poem, for example, he rebuked him for having chosen a romantic reason for his hero's becoming a Volga boatman and not a sociological, that is, typical reason. He objected to the search for the exceptional and preferred in poems on subjects such as the *burlaki* the characteristic and representative to the individual and particularizing.

25. Victor Erlich writes: "The Symbolist movement was the swan song of that part of the Russian intelligentsia which was drawn from the gentry or upper middle class." He considers Alexander Blok the greatest poet of a movement which thought that "Poetry is a revelation of ultimate Truth, a higher form of cognition, capable of bridging the gap between empirical reality and the 'Unknown.'" *Loc. cit.*, pp. 16; 18.

26. V. Briusov and A. Bely, the chief theoreticians of the Symbolist school, made important contributions to an understanding of Nekrasov's artistry.

27. In the following brief outline we rely mainly on Victor Erlich's book, with some minor differences of opinion. A fine summary of Eikhenbaum's views is given on page 237.

28. A whole chapter devoted to Lenin's use of Nekrasov may be found in Chukovsky's *Books and People*, p. 391 f.

Selected Bibliography

1. WORKS

Nekrasov, N. A. *Complete Works and Letters,* ed. V. E. Evgen'ev-Maksimov, A. M. Egolin, and K. I. Chukovsky. Moscow: Gosizdat, 1948–53. 12 vols. All references in the text are to this critical edition. Variant readings and critical commentary, identifications of persons and references make this indispensable for scholarly use. This is now the standard text; other editions, perhaps more readily available, are listed below.

———. *Works.* Moscow: Goslitizdat, 1959. 3 vols.

———. *Selected Works.* Moscow: Gosizdat, 1962. 2 vols.

2. BIOGRAPHIES

Evgen'ev-Maksimov, V. *The Life and Works of N. A. Nekrasov.* Moscow-Leningrad: Goslitizdat, 1947–52. 3 vols. Painstakingly thorough even in trivia. Indispensable but boring. Strange omissions of details of private life. Full of factual information, but dull and stereotyped in evaluations. Unfinished; takes the poet up to 1868.

———. *The Creative Career of N. A. Nekrasov.* Moscow-Leningrad: Academy of Sciences, 1953. A shorter version of the above. Useful reference.

Pypin, A. *N. A. Nekrasov.* St. Petersburg, 1905. The first full work on Nekrasov still of interest to the modern reader. Pypin sees literature primarily from the point of view of social development; considers Nekrasov as the heir of Gogol and the natural school.

Stepanov, N. L. *N. A. Nekrasov.* Moscow: Goslitmuzei, 1947. A popularizing sketch of his life and works.

3. TRANSLATIONS

Cornford, Frances and Salaman, Esther. *Poems From the Russian.* London: Faber & Faber, 1948. A few poems by Nekrasov.

Jarintzov (Zharintsov), N. *Russian Poets and Poems.* New York, 1917. Quaint English at times.

Soskice, Juliet M. *Who Can Be Happy and Free in Russia?* London: Oxford University Press (1917). A serious attempt to preserve most of the prosodic features of the original and proof that it cannot be done.

Poems by Nicholas Nekrasov. London: Oxford University Press (1936). Includes "Russian Women," "The Pedlars," "Red-nosed Frost," "Vlas," "The Railway," and others. Lively efforts.

A Treasury of Russian Verse, ed. Avrahm Yarmolinsky, New York, 1949. Four pages devoted to Nekrasov.

Wiener, Leo. *Anthology of Russian Literature, Part II.* New York, 1903. A few short poems and brief selections from "Red-nosed Frost" and "Who Lives Happily in Russia?"

General Histories

Mirsky, D. S. *A History of Russian Literature.* New York, 1934. Repeats most of the slanders about Nekrasov and many of the standard misunderstandings.

Ovsianikov-Kulikovsky, D. N. *Collected Works,* Volume VII, Part 1. St. Petersburg, 1910. The section entitled "The History of the Russian Intelligentsia" is an interesting account of the intellectual movements of the nineteenth century. His primary interest is in what he calls "socio-psychological" types, bold classifications, and interesting profiles.

Paggioli, Renato. *The Poets of Russia.* Cambridge: Harvard University Press, 1960. Very good survey.

Pypin, A. N. *The History of Russian Literature.* 4th edition, St. Petersburg, 1913. Volume IV. Nekrasov is studied in a section called "After Gogol."

Slonim, Marc. *The Epic of Russian Literature.* New York: Oxford University Press, 1964. Very good survey, good section on Nekrasov. Bibliography includes translations into English.

The History of Russian Literature. Volume IV, Part II; ed. Alekseyev. M. P. Moscow-Leningrad: Academy of Sciences, 1956. Detailed study of the period, much valuable information, and a general evaluation couched in party-line jargon.

5. SPECIAL STUDIES

Berlin, Isaiah. "A Marvellous Decade" in *Encounter,* IV, V, VI, 1955–56. A marvelous essay on the 1840's.

Monas, Sidney. *The Third Section.* Cambridge: Harvard University Press, 1961. A fascinating study of "Police and Society in Russia under Nicholas I." Bibliography.

Tompkins, Stuart Ramsay. *The Russian Mind.* Norman: University of

Oklahoma Press, 1953. From Peter the Great through the Enlightenment. Intellectual history; considers the press, censorship, influence of philosophical schools.

Venturi, Franco. *Roots of Revolution.* Translated from the Italian by Francis Haskell, New York: Alfred Knopf, 1960. The subtitle, *A History of the Populist and Socialist Movements in Nineteenth Century Russia,* gives no hint of the wealth and competency of this remarkable book.

6. LITERARY STUDIES

Chukovsky, Kornei. *The Mastery of Nekrasov.* 4th edition, Moscow: Gosizdat, 1962. The best single study of Nekrasov's art. Careful study of his relation to Pushkin and Gogol, followed by detailed and perceptive analyses of his style and usages. Documents the occurrences of key words, corrects many errors. Establishes Nekrasov's principles of composition by intensive study of the variant readings.

———. *Books and People.* Moscow: Gosizdat, 1958. Interesting studies of people around Nekrasov and special studies of themes in Nekrasov.

Egolin, A. M. *Nekrasov and the Democratic Poets of the 1860's to the 1880's.* Moscow: Gosizdat, 1960. Valuable study of Nekrasov's work. Important study of his successors.

Eikhenbaum, B. M. *On Literature.* 'S-Gravenhage: Mouton & Co., 1962. Photomechanic reprint of the Leningrad edition of 1924. A collection of fifteen essays, the last of which is devoted to Nekrasov. Represents an important breakthrough in the study of Nekrasov; influenced later Soviet critics.

Erlich, Victor. *Russian Formalism.* 'S-Gravenhage, 1955. A fine study which gives much more than the title promises. Deals with earlier historians of literature, the Symbolist movement, and other schools before presenting the Formalists.

Evgen'ev-Maksimov, V. E. *Seminar on Nekrasov.* Leningrad: Leningrad University Press, 1955. Bibliography, problems for study, special topics, brief history of texts and criticism, chronology of life and works. Useful reference.

Nicholas Alekseyevich Nekrasov, ed. M. M. Kalaushin. Moscow: Gosizdat, 1955. An illustrated chronology of his life and works.

Continuity and Change in Russian and Soviet Thought, ed. Ernest J. Simmons. Cambridge: Harvard University Press, 1955. A collection of essays by experts in different fields. Of especial interest to students of Nekrasov's age are the essays by Rufus W. Mathewson, Jr., "The Hero and Society: The Literary Definitions" (1855–

1865, 1934–1939), p. 255 f., and by René Wellek, "Social and Aesthetic Values in Russian Nineteenth-Century Literary Criticism," p. 381 f.

7. COLLECTIONS

Literary Heritage, 3 vols. Moscow: Academy of Sciences, 1946–49. Special studies, biographical material, letters, biographical studies. Much of the material is now contained in the apparatus of the critical edition.

Nekrasov Collection, 3 vols. Moscow-Leningrad: Academy of Sciences, 1951–60. Valuable special studies, source studies, and notes.

The History of Russian Criticism, Vol. I, Moscow-Leningrad: Academy of Sciences, 1958. The Soviet view of all the famous critics of the nineteenth century, with an interesting section on Nekrasov.

8. ESTHETICS AND PROSODY

Lavretsky, A. *The Esthetic Views of Russian Writers.* Moscow: Gosizdat, 1963. A collection of articles on some major writers of the nineteenth century.

Unbegaun, B. O. *Russian Versification.* London: Oxford Press, 1956. Very valuable study of the principles of Russian prosody, lucidly presented in English with Russian equivalents and many examples.

9. JOURNALISM

Zapadov, A. V. *The History of Russian Journalism.* Moscow: Gosizdat, 1963. The periodicals of the eighteenth and nineteenth centuries, with statistics, brief biographies, accounts of the feuds, data on censorship.

10. MEMOIRS

Annenkov, P. V. *Literary Memoirs.* Moscow: Gosizdat, 1960. Slightly overemphasizes Turgenev's role in *The Contemporary.* The notes and introduction correct some of Annenkov's errors, notably in his account of Turgenev's break with Nekrasov in 1860.

Panayev, I. I. *Literary Memoirs.* Moscow: Gosizdat, 1950. Introduction and notes by I. Iampol'sky. Personal glimpses of Nekrasov, Belinsky, and many others in the St. Petersburg of the 1830's and 1840's. Much gossip, some superficial views, but also interesting opinions about figures.

Panayeva, A. Ia. *Memoirs.* Moscow: Gosizdat, 1956. Introduction and notes by K. Chukovsky. Interesting reading; much gossip; many tales of interesting people; very feminine and slanted views of personalities like Turgenev, Annenkov, Botkin, Belinsky, Dobroliubov; and a "domestic" view of Nekrasov. The notes and introduction correct errors, supply biographical information, and explain references.

11. OTHER AUTHORS

Riurikov, B. *N. G. Chernyshevsky*. Moscow: Gosizdat, 1961. A survey of his life and works; includes his novels as well as his critical writings.

Dostoyevsky, F. M. *The Diary of a Writer*. Translated by Boris Brasol. New York: George Braziller, 1954. Important annotations.

Solov'ëv, G. *The Esthetic Views of N. A. Dobroliubov,* Moscow. Library of Belles-Lettres, 1963. Summary of his views, growth of his concept of realism.

Index

77108

DATE DUE

891.7
N418P
77108
AUTHOR
Peppard, M B
TITLE
Nikolai Nekrasov. (TWAS, 19)

DATE DUE	BORROWER'S NAME

891.7
N418P
Peppard, M B
Nikolai Nekrasov. (TWAS, 19)

OHIO DOMINICAN COLLEGE
LIBRARY
COLUMBUS, OHIO 43219

DEMCO